The Mystery of the Two Margarets

Margaret Bezan and Margaret Atwood

Edward Fullbrook

Literary Fiction Ltd

Cover image: Vyacheslav Argenberg, Wikicommons

Contents

Part I: Margaret Bezan

Hello world

Happy Acre subversion

This is the story of how someone I knew non-romantically and outside any social-economic structure and only for a month and a bit and not all that well and much less well than I thought, completely changed my life from what it would have been if I had not known her. For you the reader there is a downside to this story in that before we get to its heart, I need to tell you quite a bit about nobody-me so that you can see how it was that this woman subverted the then Edward and turned his life into one he had never imagined.

I'm a bit shy about telling the story because due to the mystery that surrounds it, you are only the second person to whom I've told the story.

****

THE MYSTERY OF THE TWO MARGARETS

I can't find Antigua's Happy Acre Hotel on Google Earth. Like most things of half-a-century ago, it's probably gone and forgotten. It consisted of two wooden buildings, and the one I lived in was old and rotting with a broad two-story covered veranda on three sides. The story I am about to tell is the story of how me reading a novel led me to know a woman there in 1964 named Margaret, and how me knowing her led me to read another book that fundamentally changed my life and how the morning Margaret and I said goodbye she offered me a strategy for living that later saved my life and how years later I came to ask who that Margaret in Antigua really was. I knew her only platonically. If you don't count the time I started to get an erection when she was sitting on my lap, the closest we came to physical intimacy was one evening when we were smoking cannabis together. We had been part of a group of six or seven until the others left Dado's Happy Acre room for the midnight sub-tropical breezes on the upper veranda. Margaret and I were sitting side-saddle next to each other on Dado's bed when a worried look came across her face. She had her right hand cupped over her left breast.

"I shouldn't smoke marijuana. It makes my heart palpitate."

She took her hand away from her heart and started to take hold of my hand, presumably to let me too feel her irregular heartbeat. Then she had second thoughts.

A sex manual

In 1952, Blanch Knopf, cofounder in 1915 with her husband of the publishing house Alfred A. Knopf, Inc, was in Paris looking for French books to publish in English. One of the

2

books for which she bought the English rights was Simone de Beauvoir's *The Second Sex*. Knopf's purchase, however, was based on a huge misunderstanding. She thought *The Second Sex* was a sex manual written by a woman well-known for her fondness of sex.

Back in New York, Blanch and Alfred became worried that the French woman's sex manual would not make it past the American censors. So they hired a well-known Smith College zoologist with an interest in human sexuality to translate the sex manual and to write a scholarly introduction.

The book's translator, H. M. Parshley, soon realized that it was not a sex manual that he was translating, but something more serious, and he informed the Knopfs. They told him to continue.

When the book was ready to be published, the Knopfs became worried that the book would not sell well, and certainly (or so they thought) not as well as it would if it really were a sex manual. So, since they no longer had anything to fear from the censors, they decided to go ahead and market it as if it were a sex manual.

Without this decision of the Knopfs, my life would have been unrecognizable from what it has turned out to be. But it was Margaret at Happy Acre in Antigua who made the Knopf's marketing decision life-determining for me.

Ernest Hemingway and my Aunt Helen

I grew up and went to university in Lincoln, Nebraska, USA.

My mother's older sister, Helen, had a twenty-year career as a spy that only started when she was about forty. Before that she worked in a bank in Lincoln. Her best friend was a flamboyant and exceptionally good-looking woman, Tanya, who had grown up in Lincoln speaking Russian in "Russian Town". In the late thirties, what is now called the CIA recruited this "white Russian" to pass as a "red Russian" in China. When after a couple of years she returned to Lincoln, she bought a red convertible and drove top-down around town, sometimes with my Aunt Helen.

Meanwhile Helen had married, and the US had entered the Second World War. Helen dreamed of escaping Lincoln-life and was openly jealous of Tanya's recent adventures. One summer evening cruising in the convertible, Tanya told Helen that she too could become a spy if her professor husband would become a diplomat and act as her cover. Within days Helen's husband was consulting his family's strong links with the diplomatic corps and Tanya was approaching her spy superiors. A few months later Helen's husband took up an embassy post in Montevideo and Helen went off to spy school. During the war Uruguay's capital competed with Lisbon for the title of spy capital of the world.

My Aunt Helen's last assignment was Cuba. She and her husband had been sent there when the revolutionaries were still in the mountains. A year or two after Castro's assent to power my mother received a phone call from her sister very early one morning before anyone was up. She was in Miami, she said. She had left Cuba in a speed boat in the middle of the night. Would it be alright if she came up to Lincoln to stay with us for a few weeks? This, along with meeting Margaret in Antigua, was to prove one of the big positive life-changing events of my life.

A week after Helen arrived, Ernest Hemmingway, whose history of head injuries was causing him dementia, committed suicide. Helen was a big reader and had been all her life and Hemmingway was one of the literary novelists she admired most. The day after his death, a TV network announced they were showing a late-night special hour-long program on Hemmingway's life. That was not the sort of program watched in our house, but when Helen asked me if I wanted to watch it with her, I said yes.

So, there we were in front of the little black-and-white screen and soon like Helen I was fascinated by the life Hemmingway had led, especially in his twenties in Paris, and fascinated too that like Helen he had stepped out from a modest, insular Midwestern background to lead another life. But it was what happened the next day that changed the course of my life and led me toward Margaret in Antigua. Helen made a trip to Lincoln's downtown and when she returned presented me with three Hemmingway books: *The Sun Also Rises*, *For Whom the Bell Tolls* and *Old Man and the Sea*. Immediately I read all three, and then reread *The Sun also Rises*.

Perhaps no writer has ever lived whose public image was so macho as Hemmingway's. Freudians have had a lot to say about it, but rather than make sense of Hemmingway I want to convey to you what he gave me, and this is not easy because our culture has changed so much since he died. Although my Aunt Helen was a careerist of sorts, I did not know that at the time, and if I had I would have found that nearly as improbable as the fact that it took the form of her being a spy.

In my world back then, or at least as I understood it, women only worked if their husband's earnings were thought inadequate or if they had failed to find a husband. Even today when I look back on the early-60s-Lincoln world that I knew, I can think of only one exception. Back then females lived within the limits of what men wanted, and those who showed hints of resistance were called "boyish". But that night sitting with Aunt Helen on the couch in front of the TV, I learned that Hemmingway had married four times, each time to a full-scale committed careerist, and three of them extraordinarily successful at it. Even more incomprehensible to me, he met his fourth wife in France on a battlefield where they were both working as war correspondents. These Hemmingway facts were so far beyond the range of my cultural comprehension that for me they fell in the "Ripley's Believe It or Not" category and thus were of no danger to my identity. But *The Sun Also Rises* was.

From my first reading of Hemmingway's first novel, I knew what it was that fascinated me, but I was years away from understanding why, and if I hadn't met Margaret in Antigua my understanding would have come too late to enable the good life that I have known. The *it* that fascinated me was the narrator Jake Barnes' relationship with Brett Ashly, who back then was what was called a "bitch". Jake and Brett were victims of WWI battlefields, Jake physically emasculated and now prone to fits of crying in the middle of the night, and Brett emotionally damaged from years of nursing in military hospitals and now hypersexual and aggressively promiscuous. Despite her man's haircut, she had men at every Paris café falling in love with her. But it was neither Brett's sexuality nor Jake's unavailability for it that fascinated me, but rather the way Jake thought of and talked with this woman as his existential equal. I had never knowingly encountered, even in fiction, this type of relationship between a man and a woman.

I, like Brett, was by the standards of my day abnormal when it came to my relations with the opposite sex. All the time I was growing up I had spent more time playing and socializing with girls and had more friendships with girls and, come adolescence, deeper sexual experiences with girls than did other boys. But when I was fifteen-and-a-half, all that reversed. The impromptu, on-the-street, no-adult neighbourhood life in which I had so enjoyed the opposite sex came to a complete end. Now, outside of home life, there was only school life and the relations that grew out of it. But for me, I soon discovered, those relations included none with girls, because I was now deeply ill at ease with girls and they with me, and I had no idea why. But this incompatibility continued, and as the years began to pass it increasingly brought me unhappiness. In university I had had a thousand heterosexual fantasies, but I graduated with far more credits than I had had dates, and that pattern continued into graduate school.

When I read *The Sun Also Rises*, although I was twenty-two, less than half a year had passed since when for the first time ever I had read a book with enjoyment. (I will explain later why it took so long.) At the time I was an economics graduate student. I had organized some of my peers into a discussion group that once a month met in one of our basement apartments with a case of beer and a guest professor. One month our guest was a young professor whom I liked and who was soon to make millions off his Economics 101 textbook. Halfway through our case of beer someone asked him, "What do you do if after you've been working on your dissertation for a year or

7

longer you discover that the data you've collected doesn't support your hypothesis?" "You reselect the data", was his answer. "How do you do that?" someone asked. The professor volunteered to hold a short series of seminars to show us how to game the stats. When the time came for the first one, I couldn't make myself go. My peers came away from the seminar enthused. Likewise for the second and third. I decided economics was not for me.

Without that hour on the couch with Helen and Hemmingway, I don't doubt that I would have suppressed my disillusionment and continued with life as a graduate student. But the possibility of a Jake-Barnes-life as I fantasized it now made daily noises in the back and increasingly in the fore of my mind, and I had recently come into a go-traveling-abroad-size sum of money. It took most of a year to screw up my courage, but I finally succeeded and set off from Nebraska with a backpack a quarter full of books to see a bit of the world.

Transfixed

Sometimes small bad fortunes later become good fortunes. My first eight weeks traveling in Europe with a fraternity brother on a Vespa were fascinating but not identity changing. Then my friend returned home, and I was traveling on my own and I wasn't very good at it.

After a short trip to Germany to visit a Nebraska friend at an American military base, and a few days in boring Belgium, I crossed the channel and went on up to London, where I then had most of the day to find myself a bed for the night. But it was the weekend of the annual auto show, and every B&B and cheap hotel was full. I lacked the sense to go to a youth hostel, and, come midnight, I was bed-less and on my own.

Someone told me that the Waterloo train station stayed open all night, and about one I arrived there hoping to find a bench to lie down on. But they were all occupied by drunks and the homeless. About six – by now I had found a bench to sit on – a bobby passing through on his rounds took a kindly interest in me. He said that on the Strand on the other side of the river there was a café that opened about now, and he directed me to a hidden foot bridge that crossed the Thames. It was still deep night, and except for one staggering man I walked the whole way there, a least a mile, without seeing anyone.

But the café, which sat over 50, was packed with shabby and smelly men who – the bobby had told me – were newspaper venders. They welcomed me and made room for me on a bench at the back. After my night at Waterloo, it was a good place to be, and I had my first ever tea with milk and two horrible pastries.

When I left the café, it was still night. Except for the occasional black taxi, the centre of London was lifeless. I walked up the Strand to Trafalgar Square. No one, not a single soul except me was there. I don't know for how long I stood there transfixed by this improbable solitude. Then ever so slightly dawn began to glimmer, and I heard them before I saw them. Ruffling their feathers. Pigeons. Hundreds, maybe thousands of pigeons began flying from one rooftop ledge to another, back and forth across the vast empty square. It was full daylight when I left.

THE MYSTERY OF THE TWO MARGARETS

On the edge

That first time I was in London for a week, and I left it depressed. I was both lonely and beginning to worry, more than usual, about knowing who I was. I hitchhiked to Portsmouth where in a bookshop I discovered Ordinance Survey Maps, bought one of the Isle of Wright, caught the ferry there and spent four days walking around the island on footpaths. That lifted my spirits a bit but not my sense of identity. Returning to the mainland, I hitched west to dismal Plymouth and then further west to Penzance, only a few miles from Land's End. It was midafternoon and cold and windy. I was sitting on a public bench on the harbor's edge. A group of children in school uniforms were passing by, a few dockers were hanging around, a flock of seagulls was swirling about, and I felt like I had never been so alone in all my life. Loneliness had first grabbed me hard when I was in London. I had made the mistake of staying in a cheap hotel instead of a youth hostel. Now I was not only lonely, but also the excitement of being in foreign lands had worn off, and I was, maybe not clinically, but seriously depressed. And each day a bit more than the day before. One morning I realized I no longer had any story to tell myself about where I was going in life and that soon I really wouldn't even know who I was.

But now there I was, such as I was, in Penzance, and there was nowhere for me to go until the youth hostel, which was out beyond the edge of town, opened in the evening. It was overcast, and the sky was turning darker. A couple of small ships were in, and I just sat there alone on the bench gazing out at the vast grey sea. And then gazing and gazing, I began to worry about how deep my depression was getting. I remembered the booklet I'd bought at a newsstand, *The Isles of Scilly*, and dug it out of my backpack. An archipelago off the Cornish coast, it said. Covered in heathland and fringed by sandy beaches ... 145 islands, 5 inhabited. Has a total population 2,096. 96% of the inhabitants born in the islands. I read these details and lots more and started reading them again, but then I couldn't read them anymore nor look at the map nor even fantasize about going to the isles. Sitting there I thought maybe, like Jake Barnes in *The Sun Also Rises*, I was going to cry. Sometimes you can feel so lost, and there on the bench I couldn't keep away from thinking how lost I was. I no longer had any idea where my future might be. Nor did I have anyone to turn to for moral support. Even if I went back to where I came from, I could no longer be who I had been, and I didn't know where I might go instead. Maybe it's dangerous, I thought, my being so close to the sea like this. I stood up, put on my backpack, and walked inland and then up and down the main street until it got to be dinnertime. When I came to a brightly lit diner but thinking of the harbor's edge, I had last-supper thoughts as I went in. The diner was crowded, and the waitress made me share a table with a middle-aged traveling carpet salesman.

My luck had turned. Through the whole dinner, the salesman, who I am sure sensed that he was table-sharing with someone teetering on the edge, talked to me non-stop about carpet selling. We both had apple crumble for dessert. When we finished, he gave me his business card, and we stood up and shook hands, and I thanked him for being such a good dinner companion. I should have thanked him for saving my life.

The Isles of Scilly

Outside the rain had arrived. Compared to how I had been, I was now, thanks to the carpet salesman, in good spirits, and I soon found the lane leading to the youth hostel. The map said it was two miles out of town. The lane was narrow, high-hedged, unlit and, except for me, deserted. It was an English rain, gentle but steady. There were gaps in the clouds and occasionally moonbeams danced on the blacktop in front of me. I was liking this walking alone in the dark in this rain, and although the countryside was invisible, it was pungent with the wet, and my backpack wasn't heavy, and I was wearing an army poncho. The bottoms of my jeans were getting soaked, but I didn't mind because I could feel the walk doing me good. For a while I pretended that I was the only person in the whole world.

Then I could smell the youth hostel. The waitress back at the diner had said I would. I hadn't seen it yet, but I could hear the pigs oinking. I came around a bend in the driveway and there in front of me, faintly distinguishable, were the outlines of a tall house with a pointed roof. The driveway became a path, and behind the low fences on both sides of me the pigs, barely visible in the dark, oinked and lumbered about. Except for a faint light in a lower window, the big house was in darkness.

I was beginning to think no one was home when the door opened. It was the warden. I could see he was tall, but the porch and the entrance hall were unlit, and I couldn't see his face. He invited me in. I followed him up to a registration counter and a tiny, red-shaded lamp that made his face visible as a pinkish blur. The air quality had improved more than the light. I signed a form and the warden handed me back my youth-hostel card.

"You'll find two nice Aussie lasses in the common room through that door."

****

It must have been the smallest common room in the British Isles. The two lasses were reading. One was slightly chubby but pretty, the other not pretty but shapely. Both looked early-to-mid-twenties. The room was so small it consisted only of its four corners. By the time I had occupied my corner and sat down in a squeaky chair and pulled out my Scilly Isles booklet, the three of us had spoken a total of six syllables, each of us the same two.

In my corner there was so little light that I soon felt foolish pretending to be reading.

"Where are you coming from?" was my opener.

"London," said the pretty one. "We hitchhiked down."

"Me too. I came along the south coast"

"We're going back that way," said the other.

"I'm thinking of going to the Isles of Scilly. Do you know about them?"

They didn't, but soon did. I bombarded them with Scilly facts and showed them the map and told them I had seen a sign down on the wharf saying that a ferry to the Isles left the next morning at ten. The pretty one was from Sidney, the shapely one from Tasmania, and they were both nurses working at the same London hospital. I was mystified by how relaxed we were with each other, and less than an hour after our hellos we decided we would catch that ferry.

THE MYSTERY OF THE TWO MARGARETS

****

I expected that in the morning when I came down for breakfast the nurses would tell me they had changed their minds. Instead, they were worried we would miss the ferry.

I hadn't told them that the passage to the isles was notoriously rough, but we all kept our breakfast down, and midafternoon we staggered ashore and found our way to a primitive bed-and-breakfast a mile out from the isles' only town. I was increasingly mindful of the pleasure my new companions were giving me, but it was not until we were having a pint in the Bishop & Wolf that it dawned on me that they were competing for my affection and possibly more.

I waited till the next evening to make my choice, who, the next morning engineered it so that we all missed the thrice-weekly ferry.

The gift of a smile

A week later I arrived back in London feeling ludicrously exhilarated. I checked into the Holland Park youth hostel and immediately started making acquaintances from various countries, some of whom joined me on my explorations of London. But it was what happened – *almost nothing* – one evening in the youth hostel's dining room that made me think that for unknown reasons my fortune in life had maybe changed fundamentally. It was about nine o'clock. Dinner was long finished, and seventy or eighty international travelers, nearly all in their twenties, were conversing around the long dining tables. Among the seventy or eighty of us, I counted six women. Two were sitting next to each other at the table where I was sitting. One was pretty and the other verged on beautiful. Six or seven of us young men were crowded around their table, competing for their attention. I had also sat at their crowded table the previous evening, and tonight at their invitation I was sitting directly opposite them. Oddly, they were from the same or almost the same place as me, Omaha, Nebraska. No young women from Nebraska and, prior to Penzance, no young women from anywhere had ever treated me like this or given me this kind of relaxed but cerebral pleasure. Both were rather literary, and the beauty, who was also jokey, was light-heartedly leading our conversation about novels.

But I had only started reading novels after my evening with Helen and Hemmingway. So my contributions to the conversation were limited and probably philistine. Even so, the two Omahans, who were returning home the next day, were giving me more eye contact than anyone else. They seemed glad for my company, and I was completely at ease when I mentioned that I had read *Appointment in Samarra* by John O-Hara. "Oh", said the beautiful one, "my mother reads *him*." This, as intended, got a laugh. But then smiling, and it was a big warm smile, she looked me in the eyes, and I read her smile as saying, "I can tease you a little, because we're friends." That's what back then I believed she was saying to me, and I still do. And as soon as her eyes left mine, I broke off mental contact with our table and looked around at the big room with its twelve-to-one ratio of young men to young women. For the second night in a row, I was one of the favored few and enjoying it, and there had been the two Australian nurses and after them a slow relaxed conversational stroll with a young

German woman from the hostel in Oxford. All this in the space of a fortnight and all upside-down from how my life had worked since I was fifteen and a half. I looked again and again around the big dining room and thought: WHAT THE HELL HAS HAPPENED?

It would be two years before I would figure it out, and then only because of Margaret.

Escape

Retardation

A strange thing about one's past is that you become more intimate with parts of it as you grow older because of what you have learned. Vantage points that once were inaccessible become reachable, and you hear, often when you wake up in the middle of the night, previously missing parts of the story of who you really are. When I was twenty-one, I still could not have coherently told you the true story of my growing up. And writing this little book about the two Margarets, I thought maybe I could get away without telling the story to you. If I had told it at the very beginning you might have stopped reading, but maybe now I have gained just enough of your confidence so that you won't.

THE MYSTERY OF THE TWO MARGARETS

What I need to tell you about is that at the age of five I was classified as borderline mentally retarded. And who knows, officially I may still be. But at the age of fifteen and a half I engineered a partial escape, and then beginning when I was 22 I escaped a bit more, and then finally when I was 37 I escaped completely.

There is a ludicrous irony to my retardation story. I remember being taken at the age of four to an isolated office block and up an elevator to a tiny room where a woman asked me questions. My parents wanted to start me in school a year early, but not for the reasons you would think. And I must have given the right answers, because I started school five months after my fourth birthday.

****

Kindergarten went fine. But at the beginning of first grade, I became aware of a change-of-fortune. We sat at long low tables drawing things – I don't remember what – with the teacher circulating behind us, peering down over each child's head and then, more often than not, leaning over and scribbling a red star on the child's paper. I watched most of my classmates receive red stars every day, and as the weeks passed I realised I was the only one who had received none. One morning I broke down. I knew that my classmates took home their red-starred papers to show their parents. That morning with a red crayon I drew a star on one of my papers and at lunchtime took it home and showed my mother.

Of course my mother instantly recognized that the red star had been drawn by her five year old son. And she couldn't have been nicer about it. Today I can still hear her voice, "Don't worry my darling; you'll get a red star." And I did, but not for ten years and as those years passed, she and my father went along with the school system's unchanging assessment of my capabilities. There were, as my parents' daily conversation implied, the "bright" boys and girls I played and went to school with and there was me. It wasn't until I was fifteen and a half that the school system began to revise its opinion of me. My father, however, onto his deathbed disputed the revision.

****

Once a week from the second through the sixth grade a special teacher turned up at our school and I along with two others were given special treatment. One was Judy, whom I remember with affection.The other was Norman, a fostered boy who later was institutionalized. Each week the special teacher would interrupt our class, and Judy, Norman and me would be led away and down into the basement. I remember nothing about those sessions except the tiny dimly lit windowless room and the expression of pity hanging on the special teacher's face, and the stares of my 25 classmates each week as I stood up to leave the classroom and two hours later as I crept back to my desk.

By the time I left primary school and entered seventh grade in Irving Junior High School with 750 students I really was, school-wise, retarded. My reading speed was less than half what it should have been, my vocabulary miniscule and my written sentence construction non-existent. My new school had three academic tracks, so instead of being in the basement two hours a week, I was there two or three hours every day and, except for Judy and Norman, well-segregated from my former classmates. Even my assigned locker was down in the basement in a corner reserved for troublemaking and/or especially dumb boys like me.

****

Beginning when I was ten there was a year-long series of family events that suggests a subplot to my destiny. My father was a professor of marketing, and in his study at home on the top of his rarely accessed bookcase was a small trophy, a bronze cup engraved "Checkers Champion of Iowa University 192?". When I was ten, he introduced me to the game, and soon we were playing most evenings after dinner. Checkers, or draughts as the Brits call it, is a natural handicap game. In the beginning my father would start off with nine or ten fewer pieces than me. Then as the games became closer, he would reduce the handicap by one. After we had played like that for about a year, the handicap was only one and then none and then one evening I won. My father never played checkers or any other game with me again.

One morning a few months after my win, my father was giving me a ride to school when he stopped to give a lift to two hitchhiking students. Dad recognized one of the boys whose father was also a professor. The boy, in the same year as me, said he was enjoying a new club that his father and some other professors had set up to teach their sons chess. That evening I asked my father if he would arrange for me to join this club.

"No, it wouldn't be right for me to do that. You have to be smart to play chess. You'd only embarrass yourself," he said.

****

I entered Lincoln High School with a nine-year history of retardation, and no one believed in its legitimacy more than me. More painful was the ostracization in school by those who once, before my three years in the junior high school basement, had been my peers and my friends. The possibility that I might never finish high school had been raised at the family dinner table, and my greatest fear now was what would happen to me in my junior year when I would have to take a "literature" course. How could I ever pass a course named with a mysterious four-syllable word?

Ed-in-the-neighbourhood

But I've misled you a bit. Well in fact, rather a lot. I've made those nine years (and there's another one to follow) sound worse than they were, because I have told you only about the bad side of my change-of-fortune. The good side is the perverse way I dealt with it. I split Edward, or Ed as I was then known, into two persons, Ed-in-school and Ed-in-the-neighbourhood. To explain this, I need to go back and tell you something about my life before I started school.

As I told you, they started me in school a year early. But not because I was perceived as especially bright, but because my parents wanted me out of the house, and it would also save them money because they would no longer have to pay Josephine to come every day to look

21

after me. It was this wanting me out of the house and out of their way that saved and eventually, with Margaret's help, made my life.

From the time I was an advanced toddler I was encouraged to go out and roam. There is a large scar on the inside of my right wrist that led girlfriends in my youth (the nurse from Tasmania was one) to believe I had once attempted suicide. But the scar is merely the consequence of a three-year-old's early morning exploration. Josephine hadn't arrived yet, and to my parents' relief I had gone out to explore the neighborhood, and a neighbor's broken concrete birdbath had crashed down on me. Lots of blood, but no damage to my spirit.

****

When I was five, they gave me a wristwatch and taught me how to read it. The watch's function was to enable me to arrive home for dinner at exactly 5:40. I was long past the days when I needed encouragement to go out and roam. Now outside of home and school I lived in a make-believe world. When the school bell rang at 3:15, I was out the door a minute later. Immediately, I switched worlds. And at 6:20 when I had finished clearing the dinner table, I shot out our back door. Out there in our neighborhood I *pretended* I was as intelligent as Bob, Dick, Sara, Carol Anne, Allan, Sally, Bruce, Bill, Mickey, Cathy, Ellen, Jim, Bobby, Susan, George and all the others. And I loved it: being out there in our neighborhood and of average intelligence. It was glorious. The most beautiful neighborhood in the whole world I believed. My primary school's huge playgrounds with long banks of shrubs to hide in and trees to climb were only a block away. All around us the streets were elm-shaded, traffic-free, and there mainly, we thought, for us children to gather and play in. I trespassed with impunity into people's yards, front and back, and for blocks around knew the children of all ages and the names of their cats and dogs. Behind the houses across the street from mine were open fields running down to the Rock Island train tracks and, just beyond, a little-used city park. Because from toddlerhood onwards I had been encouraged to get out and explore, I was more adventurous and self-reliant than my playmates, and I organized them into games, pranks, and fort-building and sometimes on Saturdays led them on expeditions out of town on the Rock Island tracks. As I came to my early teens, I organized the boys into a football team and a league for it to compete in, and then a club to build a clubhouse in which we, me especially, did all kinds of things.

Each afternoon as the school door closed behind me, Ed-in-the-neighborhood stepped self-consciously out into that other world. There was no organization out there except what I provided. And no adults, no basement and no red stars, and it was in that open world with its impromptu life that I formed the other me. In the beginning the split was unintentional, but from the second or third grade on it wasn't, and each year the disconnection, the difference and eventually the incomprehension between me and me grew.

****

In classrooms I daydreamed. I had no tendency toward masochism, and daydreaming was my way, and a fairly effective one, of avoiding the humiliation that was, and I presume still is, persistently doled out in the classroom to the "retarded" or "underachievers" or however we are labelled. And the more I daydreamed, the more retarded I became.

****

Now that I have revealed my mental retardation, or at least my own and my society's belief in it, I can unveil this book's underlying structure. It is the story of how I overcame not just one but three large false beliefs, and how the overcoming of each was interdependent with overcoming the other two. How was this three-way overcoming achieved? Certainly not by any intellectual heroics by me, but rather by *the generosity and thoughtfulness of various nobodies* who passed – some only for minutes – through twenty-three years of my life, none more significantly than a woman I knew in Antigua and who introduced herself to me as Margaret Bezan.

First red star

For upwards of a decade, my two-me, two-world existence was stable. But then, inevitably, it crashed. I don't know what it is like today, but back then when one entered senior high school one's neighborhood life ended, if it hadn't already done so. Thanks to that clubhouse, which was behind the double garage in someone else's back yard, I kept mine going for another year with the help of neighborhood girls. But when I closed the door on the clubhouse for the last time, I wondered how much longer my life would continue. I really was retarded now and my other me was nearly dead, and my father had started threatening to send me away to "reform school" because of my occasional insubordination at the dinner table. And then at the beginning of my junior year – it was on the third day of classes – I had *the greatest piece of good luck in my whole life*, even greater than meeting Margaret in Antigua.

It was in the dreaded "literature" course, American Literature. On the first day as I walked into Miss Montgomery's classroom it was immediately obvious that she was some kind of a deviant. Not only were the student desk rows at a 45-degree angle to the room's walls, they also faced away from the teacher's big desk, that symbol of authority, which was out of sight at the back of the room. She was sixty-plus and had a face, a scary face, that suggested she would prefer to die than be submissive to anyone. Her description of what we were expected to do in her class terrified me. Beginning tomorrow, every day we would have to write and turn in a page or more of commentary on what we had been assigned to read. I can't remember what the first assignment was, but I gave it a go.

At the beginning of class on the third day, Miss Montgomery, cradling a fat wodge of the papers we had handed in the previous day, walked up to the front of the class. She said that before handing them back, she needed to warn us that her way of grading was non-conformist. On each paper she gave two marks instead of one. The first was for how well the paper was written; the second for how much imagination it showed.

You can see what's coming of course, but to appreciate the effect it had on me, I need – and this is going to be boring – to tell you about Lincoln High School's grading scale and my experience with it. 1 was tops and 7 failing. But the system tried to pass everyone on, including the dummies like me, so if you took the test and turned in your assignment, 6 was the bottom grade. I got lots of 6s and 5s and sometimes a 4. For me 1s and 2s were the equivalent of red stars, but by now my red star dream was ten years old and effectively dead. And red stars were light years away from my mind when Miss Montgomery handed me my folded paper and I opened it:

Composition 6

Imagination 2

Sixty-seven years later I can still see that loopy red-pencil numeral two. But at the time, rather than overjoyed, I was incredulous, so much so that for the rest of the hour I kept reopening my paper to make sure the 2 was not an illusion.

That evening after family dinner – at which I made no mention of my red star – I retired to my bedroom – now the full-extent of my neighborhood – and had a fresh look at my red star paper. Three thoughts came to mind.

1. It was obvious that Miss Montgomery, having given me a red star, was even more socially deviant than I had judged her to be on the first day. Perhaps she was a complete lunatic.

2. There were the usual red marks all over my paper, but there were also the teacher's suggestions as to how I might have written this and that differently. For me this was a novelty.

3."I am now going to write today's assignment," I told myself, "and maybe I'll get my second red star, and, what the Hell, I'll have a look at Miss Montgomery's suggestions."

A perverse decision

It was those suggestions, every school day for the next three semesters, together with the occasional red star, that beginning a year later turned my life a third of the way around. Although in my first semester with Miss Montgomery I earned a 4 and in the second a 3, in other classes my performance remained unchanged. But when I was about to start my senior year, I made a perverse decision. Just as for years in my neighborhood I had *pretended* that I was of normal intelligence, I would now *pretend* the same in school. At the beginning of my senior year, I also turned my neighborhood social skills toward school and with my new fantasy quickly acquired a small group of male friends. Also, to my delightful surprise, my fellow students were generally supportive of my fantasy. Teachers however were a mixed bag.

One day near the end of my second semester with Miss Montgomery, she had asked me what I wanted to study in university. I was astonished! But it was from that moment on that I began thinking about extending my fantasy of mental normality not just to Miss Montgomery's classroom, but to classrooms generally. In my high school everyone was required to take every semester a class called Modern Problems. For this class you kept the same teacher each year because in addition to teaching you "modern problems", they also guided your course selection and mapped your future. Miss Montgomery's subversive question led me to insist upon choosing classes that would satisfy university entrance requirements. But my Modern Problems teacher said I needed to be realistic about my abilities. When I stuck to my new fantasy and refused her suggestion that I try to become a plumber, she declared me disrespectful and self-destructive.

****

For my final year of Modern Problems, I was transferred to Mr Real who had a reputation for subduing troublemakers. By choice I occupied a corner desk at the back of the class. Mr Real was a good-looking, smooth-voiced man of forty with a kind face. On the first day, in the nicest possible way, he identified me to the class as someone who perhaps was not as gifted as they were. His classes consisted mostly of discussions of our "modern problems" reading assignments. He would ask questions and students would raise their hands if they thought they knew the answers. I knew the answers but never raised my hand. After several weeks he framed a question especially for me. The whole class turned around to see me speak. I refused. Mr Real offered me kind words of support but to no avail. Twenty minutes later Mr Real asked a question no one could answer. When he was about to give the answer himself, I shouted it out. Amusement showed on the faces of my classmates and horror on the face of Mr Real.

The next day in class I raised my hand for every question, and every time Mr Real ignored me. After a while I lost patience and started shouting out the answers. Soon my classmates were convulsed with laughter and Mr Real with anger. He ordered me out of his classroom and escorted me down to the principal's office, who fortunately was not there.

But Mr Real must have given it a think, because thereafter in class he no longer treated me as substandard, which was all I wanted. At the end of the school year, he even wished me well in university. In my memory I have liked Mr Real ever since.

****

And there was Mr. Lien. In my sophomore year he had been the teacher of my third-track English class in which he, whenever he interrupted my daydreams, forced me to play the role of the slowest-of-the-slow. Then in my last year I registered for an English grammar class he taught whose aim was to help students sit university entrance exams. He must have wondered what I was doing there, but he said nothing. The course followed a university textbook that explained English grammar in esoteric detail. Empowered with my fantasy of intellectual normalcy, I became perversely fascinated with this dullest of books. Midterm we had an exam. When it came time for Mr. Lien to hand it back, he first wrote all the 20-some exam scores on the blackboard. One was significantly higher than all the rest. He said he was sure someone had cheated on the exam, but he couldn't prove it because he didn't know how it was done. So, he was going to ask some questions before returning our papers.

He asked seven or eight students easy questions before he asked me to give an example of a subjective compliment. And I did. "That," he said, "is the one you gave on the test. Can you give me another?" I couldn't. "I see," he replied and when he left it there the message to my classmates was clear. When after class some of them approached me to tell me they didn't believe that I had cheated, it gave a big boost to my fantasy.

****

And there was Miss Roberts, a late middle-aged history teacher who once a year taught the school's only economics course, which that September I signed up for. Only twenty students turned up and, with a few exceptions, I recognized them all as the academically top students of my year. At the end of the first-day's class, Miss Roberts asked me to come and see her when school let out.

I sat down in front of her desk, and she picked up two sheets of paper and glanced at them. One I knew was my school records; the other I later learned showed my IQ score.

"I thought I should tell you that you may find my economics class more difficult than you expect."

I can't remember what I then said, but I am sure I said it with difficulty, and it was to the effect that I expected the class to be difficult but was sure I wanted to take it.

She said she could not keep me from taking it if I really wanted to, but if I changed my mind after a couple of weeks, she could arrange for me to change to another class.

I didn't change my mind, and as the semester progressed Miss Roberts encouraged me to act out my new fantasy without restraint.

Family relations

My mother faithfully worshiped respectability and, when she was ill, Jesus Christ. The former meant that her opinions about everything beyond her kitchen were those of her husband. From an early age I understood that, but of course not the culture and sociology behind it.

****

Six times a year for ten years I had been bringing home school report cards and leaving them for my father to see. Rarely did he give me any feedback, and when he did, it was of the form "not bad for you". But when in my senior year I received the first set of report cards, except for Mr. Lien and Mr. Real, all my teachers had given me twos or threes. It felt like I had fallen into a dream world, and for the first time ever I expected praise from my father for my report-cards.

My father was subject to bouts of rage, but I had never seen him so exploding with rage as when, holding my report cards, he called me into his study. He was enraged, he explained, because Mr Real had commented: "Sometimes in class he speaks out of order". I knew of course that Mr. Real's comment could not really have been the cause of my father's rage, but I was not strong enough to think about what the cause really was.

My father never mentioned my 2s and 3s.

****

Unlike my difficulties at school, I experienced those with my father as narratively unconnected events. Today it seems my good fortune that I did. If to my self-identity of being retarded, I had added being a son despised by his father who was a pilar of the community, I believe that the story I am telling you would never have come true no matter how many Miss Montgomerys and Margarets I had come to know.

****

From age two until my mid-teens, I suffered acutely from hay fever. Other children similarly afflicted were in the summer kept mostly indoors. But given my parents' taste for a child-free house and my outdoor adventurousness, this for me was not a possibility, and over the years my all-day summer rambles had a strange effect on my anatomy. Because hour after hour I repeatedly rubbed the right-side of my nose trying to subdue the violent ich, my nose grew permanently tilted to the left and with my right nostril forever blocked.

When I was fifteen, an eye, nose and ear specialist told my parents that I would gradually lose my hearing in my right ear if my nose were not straightened. It was a simple operation, requiring one or two nights in the hospital, followed by two weeks with a runny nose. But my parents decided, explained my mother, that it was not worth the money. If I wanted, I could pay to have my nose fixed when I grew up.

This decision turned out to be partially a blessing for me. Having only one functioning nostril made me exempt from the military draft.

IQ tests

At the last moment my summer job fell through, so I entered university in June, the beginning of summer school, rather than September. Within 48 hours I was summoned to a dilapidated World War II prefab belonging to the Psychology Department. This was to prove a big piece of good luck, but unlike with Miss Montgomery, goodwill was not its enabler.

When I arrived, I was ushered into a private office where a non-descript man sat behind a desk holding a yellowish sheet of paper like the one Miss Roberts was holding when she questioned my desire to take her economics course. He began by asking me a series of inane questions like "Do you perspire when you take tests?" Eventually he said they would like me to take some tests for them.

"Tests? What tests?"

"IQ tests".

"No thanks."

He said something about how it would help with the advancement of science. I said no again. He gave me a hard look and then glanced at my sheet. "I see your reading speed is worryingly low," he said. "We could speed you up."

"How?"

"Follow me and I'll show you something."

He led me to a glass cubicle at the far end of a long desk-filled office room. Inside the cubicle were four tables, four chairs and four desk-top machines. Each machine consisted merely of a rack on which you could place a large open book and over which a screen would come down and cover it up at whatever speed you set it for.

"Yes," I said, "I want to use one of those."

There was a price. I had to take at least two IQ tests, "different brands", he explained. I said okay, but not for at least two weeks.

Beginning the next day, I went into that cubicle every Monday through Friday at two and stayed until four and sometimes later. The books they provided for the machines had questions and answers at the end of each section, so you could test yourself on your reading comprehension. I could scarcely believe the progress I made. I began at 200 words a minute, which for me was speed-reading, and at the end of eight weeks I could set it at 900 and pass the tests. I also learned about taking multiple-choice tests, how to guess wrong and right answers by how they were worded.

When after three weeks and again after six, I, free of all nervousness, took an IQ test, I could read questions at what had previously been an unimaginable speed. After taking the second test, academic types came to stare at me through the glass, but, except for the secretaries, no one ever spoke to me.

In August when the university closed, I rented a typewriter and taught myself to touch-type.

Life-threatening

My ultra-slow reading speed was not the only everyday disability that had grown out of my dimwit classification. For my age my vocabulary was miniscule. In my senior year at high school, spurred on by Miss Montgomery, every week I read my parents' *Time* magazine, wrote down ten words that I didn't know and looked them up in the family dictionary. I continued this habit into university.

But when it came to the usual routines of being a university student, I was one of the most neurotic who ever existed. Remember, no one had taken me aside and said, "Sorry. we made a mistake all those formative years ago when judging you and placing you in a category." And for me – deep in my own mind – I was still in that category, and for me it was only with fantasy, like Ed-in-the-neighborhood – that each day I usually escaped it. But of course I didn't understand this, and I wouldn't until I was 37. I looked, without understanding for what it was that I was seeking, for ways to replicate that moment – still today the greatest moment in my whole life – when Miss Montgomery handed back my paper and I opened it up and saw that red star.

To test myself, I cut some classes nearly every day, week after week and never opened the textbook until a few hours before an exam. Or if it was the final then maybe the day before and I would hide away in the library stacks and cram, cram and cram. It was a contest to see how in only a few hours in a whole semester I could study and still get a B. My record was five and a half hours for a junior year course in Marketing.

But there were two or three courses, History and English, that I flunked. But not because I flunked the exams, but because I stopped going to classes completely, didn't take any exams and couldn't make myself officially "drop" the courses. Why? Because the instructor had said something to me that was life-threatening to my fantasy, and I had to block it from my mind urgently.

Knocking on an African American's door

I'm telling you the story of how nobodies passing through my life radically transformed it from what my parents, the school system and the culture of the time intended it to be. I grew up never knowingly knowing anyone who was *not* a hard-core racist. Lincoln was a northern well-educated town and there was no lynching, and no one ever talked about being a racist and if you were middle class you used the n-word "negro" instead of "nigger". But life in Lincoln was tightly segregated. Periodically the local papers published a map showing the small slum-landlord area of town where "negroes" were required to live and for whom virtually all occupations were closed. This was the society that I grew up in and that formed my beliefs, and – in so far as I can remember – I never questioned it, never dreamed of living in a world were dark-skinned people were not held to be a sub-species. But one hot summer night when I was eighteen, I encountered this dream in a friend a couple of years older than me named Biff Morison.

Five of us were sitting on the floor of the entrance hall of our vacation-empty fraternity house. Biff was a miler on the university track team. One of the team's sprinters was a Jamaican of partly African descent. When the track team went away for meets, its members shared hotel rooms. The Jamaican was the team's only non-white, and Biff was the only team member willing to share a room with him. They became good friends.

"They're human just like us," said Biff. "It's only their skin color that's different."

For that time and place it would have been virtually impossible for someone to say anything more politically incorrect. It was the first time in my life I had heard anyone proclaim that they were not a racist. The others sitting on the floor were shocked and became angry. I was shocked and became reflective.

Nine months later I was out for the university tennis team but failed to make the traveling squad when it went south on tour over spring vacation. An African American, the first one I had ever talked to, also failed to make the tour. His name was Eddie, a GI, married with two children, nearly thirty, a straight-A architecture student and, although I liked all my team-mates, I found myself chatting with Eddie the most. Now with the team heading south, I needed someone to play tennis with during the vacation.

If it hadn't been for Biff, I would not have been strong enough to ask Eddie. When I did, he looked surprised, almost shocked, and I could see him thinking about how to reply.

"Sure. Can you pick me up?"

I hadn't expected that, but I said yes, and he gave me his ghetto address.

With the family car, I pulled up in front of his sad little house and honked. I waited and then honked again. Still no Eddie. I got out of the car and climbed the broken steps to his collapsing front porch and knocked. Instantly the door opened and out shot Eddie. I'm sure he had ignored my honks so as to give me the experience of knocking on an African American's door. We played three sets and he won them all.

Escape: Stage Two

When I had entered university at seventeen, my father offered to be my advisor. I was surprised by this and gladly, but foolishly, accepted. When in my senior year I nervously mentioned to him the possibility of my going to graduate school, he said that "with a little luck" I might be admitted there at Nebraska. And I was. Then the day came when I had an appointment to see the professor who would now be my advisor.

As I sat down in front of Professor Trebing at his desk with him holding what I recognized to be a printout of my undergraduate course grades, my memory shot back to high school and Miss Roberts asking me if I really wanted to take her economics course. Then came his opening question.

"Why did you decide to stay here at Nebraska for graduate school?"

"What do you mean?"

"With these grades," and he waved the printout, "you could go anywhere. Harvard for example."

"But I didn't do well in some classes and flunked a couple."

"That wouldn't make any difference because you got straight As in economics and math and you've already taken graduate level courses."

****

As I have told you, my escape from my deep-down belief that I was mentally substandard came in three stages, beginning with my first red star. The second stage began at graduate school when I took a course taught by a Professor Peterson that focused solely on John Maynard Keynes' book *The General Theory of Employment, Interest and Money*. Until then, mine had been an all-textbook education. But there was no textbook in Peterson's course, just the original work itself. The textbook genre requires its authors to pretend to know it all and talk down to their readers. Reading *The General Theory*, I encountered for the first time an author who, like Einstein writing about physics, was openly and unashamedly struggling to understand what he was writing about. I too was struggling and so I – and what could have been more preposterous – immediately identified on an existential level with John Maynard Keynes. It meant that for the first time ever while reading a book my resentments and fears relating to my education and family receded to the background. And when they did, the most astonishing thing happened. My brain started giving me an intensity of pleasure that, except for sex, I hadn't thought possible. So it was, that an intellectual was born.

Psychological meltdown

All great books deserve to be reread. I didn't know that back then, but I had only just finished Keynes' *The General Theory* when I started reading it again. In its early pages I found a paragraph in which it looked to me that Keynes had made an error in reasoning. It had no significance for the book as a whole nor even much of it for its first part. But it had potential significance for my identity.

Over several days I reread the paragraph numerous times and reconsidered the possible meanings of its words, but to me it still appeared to contain an error of reasoning. This in no way distracted from or reduced my admiration for Keynes. Instead, it only confirmed that he, like me, was human.

Meanwhile Professor Trebing had shown one of my term papers around at a conference, and a week later I received an unsolicited offer from Wisconsin University at Madison to do a PhD there with a teaching assistantship. I was thrilled of course, but half of me, the subconscious non-fantasy me, was incredulous. It was, I think, the hope of subduing that incredulousness so that I could accept the offer, that led me up to Professor Peterson's office to show him the little mistake I had found in Keynes' book. I made him slowly read the paragraph with me, thinking that he would then see the mistake also. But despite what I had to say, he could see nothing wrong with it.

My fantasy self would probably have still been strong enough to accept the unsolicited offer from Wisconsin if the next evening I had not done something foolish. Nearing the end of dinner with my parents, I told them of the PhD offer and my intention of accepting it. My father said nothing and kept his eyes tightly focused on the slice of apple pie he had been eating. "What do you think about that?" my mother asked him. He remained silent. Then suddenly, his pie still only half eaten, he stood up, glared down at me, and said, "Do you think you're intelligent enough?" and left the room.

No words have ever damaged me so much.

****

THE MYSTERY OF THE TWO MARGARETS

When I was a small child, my parents opened a bank account for me. But of course I didn't have access to it. Every year Aunt Helen sent me a birthday check for twice as many dollars as I was old, and those checks and a few others went into my bank account.

The year I turned thirteen, I was worth over 300 dollars, and that spring I went into the lawn-mowing business. I went door-to-door to nearly a hundred houses soliciting customers and soon had a dozen regulars and by my third year more than two dozen. In the winter when it snowed, I shoveled peoples' sidewalks and driveways. Nearly all my earnings went into my bank account, and secretly I began to dream of buying a used car with my savings when I turned sixteen.

But when at seventeen I asked for access to my savings, my parents said no. I couldn't have any of my money until I was older. They waited till I was 22. But the timing couldn't have been better. After my father's six words that evening when leaving the dinner table, I had gone into psychological meltdown. But my Aunt Helen's visit had opened my eyes to the wider world, and now my childhood mowing and shoveling funded my overdue escape from my parents and Nebraska.

Travel-traveling

Examining who you are

When you reach a certain age, you look back on your earlier years and ask yourself which were the ones that most benefited all your years that followed. For me it was the two years I spent traveling. Without them, me and my life would have turned out radically different, and not nearly so good. It was from that moment in the Penzance diner when I shook hands with the traveling carpet salesman and stepped out into the cold rainy night that my traveling life really took off.

I soon realized that old Ed-in-the-neighborhood had social skills and a view of life that fitted my travelers' world. There were no hierarchies in this society and its cast of characters was constantly changing. Each day's activities required improvisation and venturing to unknown places. Groups of two and three and sometimes more needed silent leadership and I started providing it. I didn't know why me and the opposite sex were now suddenly in pleasurable harmony, but I was enjoying it, and as a traveler I was now on my feet and confident. When I left London a few weeks after my WHAT THE HELL HAS HAPENED evening in the youth hostel dining room, it was with two Canadian brothers. With the help of an East End junk dealer we had bought a retired ice-cream van. We built in some bunks, bought prima stoves and a road map, and then one night, with me driving, set off for Dover to catch the night ferry to France.

That hour back in Nebraska on the sofa with Aunt Helen and Hemmingway had been the beginning of my coming to realize that the world is a much richer place than my upbringing had led me to believe. But it had given me only a peek, only a glimmer of belief, whereas now, at the wheel of an ancient ice-cream van, suddenly there I was, and it was like I was in a dream, in another reality. Not because I was driving a strange vehicle through a dark night in an unknown land, but because I had the feeling that a new world was opening in front of me, a world that was there waiting for me to enjoy. I had never felt like that before. Gripping the van's steering-wheel and looking straight ahead, I was intoxicated with euphoria. Almost shaking. For the first time in my life, I felt free of the weight of my childhood traumas. I wasn't, of course, but sometimes ignorance is best, and in any case, I knew for certain that an unknown me was waiting for me down the road.

But much further down than I dared to guess.

THE MYSTERY OF THE TWO MARGARETS

Many of the young people I met that year and the next were in the process of examining who they were and considering how they might like to make themselves different from how their upbringing had programed them to be. In a few years this self-questioning between generations was to become common, but in 1962 it was still rare. But not among young travel-travelers. In my two years of traveling, I met and came to know scores of young people who by choice were not going to become who they had been raised to be.

When I left Nebraska, except for my Aunt Helen, I had never known anyone who had travel-traveled. When you do – I mean when day by day you move slowly on your own through alien worlds – you may see those worlds and yourself with a clarity that is addictive and sometimes frightening. And back then, more than half-a-century ago, travel-travelers found themselves in foreign lands disconnected from their roots to a degree that is virtually impossible to achieve in today's digital world. There were no mobile phones, no texting, no email, no Facebook, no Twitter, no TikTok. Except for traditional post and unaffordable "long-distance" calls, no means for family and peer-group connections existed. And there was no news-news. Even in capital cities where English newspapers were available, travel-travelers didn't buy them. Months would pass without holding one in your hands, nor did monolingual travelers like me ever hear English radio or TV. Instead, your daily life with humankind was all person-to-person.

You were also in every way but one cut off from the society that had created you. The exception was the books, usually three or four, that you carried in your backpack.

Because you could carry so few and because they were your only means of withdrawing for an hour or two from your foreign and unknown existence, and because your next three books would be obtained by trading your current books with fellow travelers, you chose your books, usually fiction, with the greatest care. I read one modern literary classic after another on my travels because that was virtually all that was available to me.

Two lessons

We had been on the road with our ice-cream van for two weeks when it broke down in the middle of almost nowhere halfway down Spain's Mediterranean coast. Luckily a repair garage was there and a café and food shop, but there was nothing to see, no local life, no seashore and nowhere to walk, and so our four-day wait there for an engine part proved memorably boring. And yet for me that breakdown was a piece of good luck, because sitting there each day on the café terrace I learned something that proved everyday useful to me over my next year-and-a-half and far beyond.

The source of my learning was an American who had recently graduated from a state university. His dream now was to go around the world. But he didn't have enough money, and he was hanging out at this nowhere, nothing-to-do-place for a couple of weeks as part of what he called his "travel training".

"I'm trying to get control of my desires," he said, and for several days he sat with us for hours on the café's terrace but never ordered anything, not even a coffee.

"I'm showing myself that my enjoyment of talking with you guys doesn't depend on my consuming coffee and wine and things. If I learn to control my desires, then I'll be able to go around the world."

****

Back then Marbella was the poshest town on the posh Costa del Sol. There was a flat bit with modern apartment buildings down by the sea and a steep half-mile of zig-zagging lanes with little red-tiled, white-washed terraced houses leading up to the town walls. Just beyond an open gate in the top wall was a stone mansion with a large swimming pool. Around the pool was a red-tiled terrace with deckchairs with a view of the Rock of Gibraltar. Sitting there I watched the big red disk set behind the rock at least a dozen times.

That mansion was now a youth hostel. That time of year, late autumn and early winter, hostellers were few. A bunk bed and three meals a day cost 60 pesetas. The official exchange rate was 56 to the dollar. Most nights there were a dozen or so of us hostellers, all male, and with most of us sleeping in what had once been someone's enormous bedroom. One night in that dormitory I learned something that more than most people I needed to learn.

I was opinionated and by now in the early stages of becoming articulate. It was perhaps the discovery that I, of all people, was becoming articulate, which led to my excess. More than listening to people, I now enjoyed arguing with them. I usually could do so without antagonizing them, but even so the object was to win the argument rather than to take in what they knew, and I didn't.

Bedtime at the hostel was early. So nearly every night when we got ourselves stuffed into our sleeping bags, conversation between bunks broke out. I turned them into debates. Then one night after I won a debate, I had a revelation: I was an idiot to have these arguments. Here I was every night and day with young people all of whom came from places and cultures and life histories different from mine and who therefore knew things that I did not know, some of which I could learn, if instead of arguing, I asked questions and listened.

Marbella enterprise

After a week in Marbella, one of the Canadian brothers, the one I had become friends with, decided he had had enough of Spain and left for Italy. His brother Ken and I each bought half of his share in the ice-cream van. Then Ken moved a few miles up the coast to live with a semi-elderly Irish earl and his young mistress, and I went into business with the van.

Gibraltar was only a 90-minute drive away. New people passed through the hostel every week, and for a reasonable fee I offered daytrips to Gibraltar. On each trip I brought back two jerrycans of gasoline which I sold to the hostel warden and several hundred dollars' worth of pesetas which I sold below the official rate to fellow travelers. Sundays I offered outings to the horrible bullfights in Torremolinos.

After a month of that I went for two weeks on the back of a Harvard graduate student's motorcycle to Morocco.

Our first night in Tangier we smoked our first cannabis, sold to us by the young youth hostel warden who showed us how to inhale deeply and hold it in. Two days later, converted, we headed south to Fès and Meknès and then up and over the Atlas Mountains and all the way down to Merzouga where if you wanted to go further south you had to switch to camels. We headed west on the motorcycle. In those days there was no real road across Morocco south of the Atlas Mountains, only a rough track leading to Marrakesh. We bounced along on it for four days, visited two kasbah towns along the way, slept rough, passed hundreds of camels and, until nearing Marrakesh, a grand total of just four vehicles.

Back in Marbella, the hostel had been invaded by the Falange. It was Franco-fascist-days in Spain, and the Falange was like the Boy Scouts except its aim was to turn boys into tomorrow's fascist underlings. Forty or fifty young Falangists and their trainers stayed several weeks at the hostel, and at every meal the dining room was stuffed with them singing and chanting. On popular demand I started up a restaurant for my fellow travelers so we could all escape from the Falangists. With the primus stoves from the van and paper plates, I cooked and served spaghetti bolognaise in the dormitory.

Toc H and Ted Joans

In today's culture if you are not a celebrity, individuality is usually understood as deviation from the norm. Last night I was rereading Konrad Lorenza's *King Solomon's Ring*. It is a book about animal behavior, and this sentence, "Personal friendship means everything to a dog," made me stop and think. What caught me was that word "personal" and the fact that its use here in the context of friendship is in Lorenza's eyes and mine too not redundant. It was when I was traveling that I came to appreciate this fact. While travel-traveling, my friendships and even acquaintance-ships were mostly with people who did not easily fit into my categories of people, and so I was forced to engage with them primarily as unique individuals. And often for the same reason they did the same with me. This two-sided daily experience, perceiving others as unique and realizing that they were doing the same with me, began to make me more aware of my own uniqueness, to see myself beyond a summation of category checklists, to intimately connect myself *existentially* with my unique past and future. My coming to identify myself primarily with my existential self was greatly helped by my friendship with the African American poet Ted Joans. It began in a bizarre place called Toc H.

After a couple of weeks of running my Marbella restaurant in the youth hostel, I was kicked out. I retrieved Ken, who by now was bored living with the Irish earl, and we drove down the coast to Gibraltar. I knew that up at the far end of its Main Street tucked between medieval fortifications was a primitive hostel called Toc H run by an elderly kilt-wearing Scotsman named Jock Brown. We hadn't been living at Toc H more than a few days when we sold our van to a local plumber for more than twice what we had paid for it in London.

It was 1963 and with few exceptions us travel-travelers came from families in which no one in peacetime had ever been abroad. Someone who came from a country different from yours came from a place whose categories of social and cultural existence were essentially unknown to you. And yours to them. This reciprocal difficulty of categorizing each other beyond the level of passports meant that every day we experienced others and saw others experiencing us as individuals in the real or existential sense to a degree we had never known before.

This was especially liberating for me, because even more that most people, I grew up perceiving myself and my dreams and fantasies in terms of socially defined categories to which I belonged or pretended to belong. But now, without yet understanding how it had happened, I was, liberated from these obsessions. I forgot, at least on the everyday level, about pretending not to be borderline mentally retarded.

****

In the evenings, Toc-H's humble common room sheltered us diverse and unknown-to-each-other travelers from the cold and rain outside. This might seem like a recipe for social disaster, but the human population is more gifted at social intercourse than its leaders, and every evening out of the initial chaos a relaxed all-inclusive civilized gathering soon emerged. The ones I remember most fondly were those informally led by "the black beatnik". That is the tag that was pinned on Ted Joans by a *Time* magazine journalist reporting on the poetry scene in 1950's Greenwich Village.

Ted was now 34, lived in Tangier, owned a house in Timbuktu, and had come to Gibraltar with his Norwegian wife for the last month of a difficult pregnancy. They were staying in a tiny house-trailer just beyond Toc-H's walls. I was aware of Ted's status as a poet because one of my first Toc-H friends told me that he had been invited to Harvard to read his poetry when she was a student there. But for me who had yet to voluntarily read a poem, and for nearly everyone else at Toc-H, Ted was, like everyone else, a nobody.

Today, over a half century later, I can still remember 30 or 40 people, some vividly, from my ten-week off-and-on (another trip to Tangier and two weeks working as a yacht-hand) stay at Toc-H. But for now, I am only going to describe Ted, the second African American to pass through my life.

Ted's parents had worked on Mississippi River boats, on one of which Ted was born. After his father was murdered in Detroit, Ted and his mother moved to Louisville, Kentucky where she worked as a maid. Sometimes after school Ted would go to the house where his mother was working and wait around until she finished. One day he opened an art book lying on a coffee table. He opened it again the next day and the next and so on, and soon he wanted to see more pictures of paintings, and he knew that there would be more books like the one on the coffee table in the town library. But because of the colour of his skin, he couldn't go into the library, let alone check out books.

Ted set about making friends with wayward white boys. Eventually he persuaded one to check out books for him. One book led to the next and eventually to fantasies about going to university and becoming a painter. Military service and the GI Bill enabled the first, and after graduating he went off to Greenwich Village and became a poet, a surrealist painter, and the only black beatnik, and then, after sharing a room with Charlie Parker, he moved to Paris where he worked as a jazz trumpeter.

With that background, Ted had no difficulty with the fact that every evening he was the only non-white in the Toc-H common room. I've never known anyone as gifted as Ted at putting people at conversational ease. But "gifted" is not quite the right word. From that first art book onwards, Ted had *learned* to experience himself as an individual in his own right, as an individual full-stop, rather than as an individual representing, for better or worse, social categories. In the daytime when he was not with his now bed-ridden wife, he engaged, often intensely, one-on-one with fellow Toc-H residents, mostly young men – German, French, Canadian, Aussie, New Zealander, Brit and American – who had probably never before conversed with a non-white. Because Ted's own identity was so much defined by his singular path through life, he tended to see other people, especially the young, in the same way, and so could become almost immediately psychologically intimate with them. Within minutes, they were telling him their dreams, and he was feeding them hope.

The Toc-H common room was a long graceless rectangle with decrepit sofas and half-broken lawn chairs. Midway down one of its long walls was a crude fireplace in which every evening a small fire burned with Ted sitting on an upturned log holding a fire-poker. As people returned from dinner at Smokey Joe's, the common room would fill up, often with people standing.

The large group conversation usually began with Ted telling a story or two from his life, not always self-flattering, and then, using knowledge gained from his daytime one-on-ones, he would draw in others, and conversation would take off in unexpected and sometimes strange directions, but always with laughter.

That social space at Toc H and among travel-travelers generally was not only unsupportive of one's usual obsession with conformity, it also made our public identities less visible and so, inevitably, our private identities more visible.

"When we're stripped of our social uniforms," said Ted one evening, "it is like we're naked." He covered his head with his jacked and people laughed.

Inexplicably, Ted and I became friends. We spent hours exploring the back alleys of Gibraltar, conversing as we walked. One afternoon – just after Ted had refused to enter a coffee shop with a sign on the door that read, "We reserve the right to refuse to serve anyone." – Ted said a few words that empowered me.

"Because of the color of my skin and what that meant to how people perceived me, I decided I would define myself from the inside-out. I would have dreams and feelings and ideas about this and that that popped into my head, and I would identify myself with those dreams and ideas and feelings, and to Hell with people's ideas about me."

It was those words that Ted gave me that day on our walk that enabled me to begin to see myself from the inside-out rather than the outside-in.

He also gave me these words of caution, "If you're conspicuously a good guy, the villains will be after you."

Ted always retired early from these gatherings to be with his wife. When he did, the group's high would collapse like a forgotten soufflé.

Then one evening Ted didn't turn up. The next morning at dawn he woke me up and pulled me out of the dorm and down into the courtyard where in the dawn light he read me the joyful poem he had written about his new-born son.

****

A couple of weeks later I spent some time with Ted in Tangier. He had returned home with his wife and new-born, and I had crossed over for a few Tangier days with a pair of Canadian nurses. One afternoon Ted showed me around his hangout spots, most of them in the casbah. The morning I was returning to Gibraltar I met him for coffee in the French quarter. When we were about to say goodbye, Ted called over a street photographer. Out of a basket he pulled two long snakes. One he wrapped around Ted's neck, the other around mine. Click. That is the photograph I most regret not having.

****

I can't remember how I found Smokey Joe's, but it was one of those places that every serious young traveler found. It was up a steep pedestrian alley off the bottom of Main Street and then down seven steps into a basement. Smokey Joe, a Spaniard who lived just across the border and walked to work every day, was usually standing behind the counter at the rear of his little subterranean greasy-spoon. After all these decades I can still see Smokey Joe standing there, see the kindness in his face, hear the humour in his broken English. Over the next few months and then a year later, I ate scores of meals there.

Rome

Near the end of February, I left Gibraltar in a VW van with its two young male Canadian owners and two young female American nurses. A week later I and the two Canadians were meandering through Madrid's vast Plaza Mayor when we encountered two eighteen-year-old girl cousins from California whom we had known at Toc H. Both were physically attractive and precociously adventurous, and one of them, Allison, would pop up again in my young life, and later through the decades, in my memory. Now they both joined us traveling in the van.

At the end of March, the seven of us, still all speaking to each other, took up residence in the centre of Rome in a sixteenth century church that had been turned into a hostel for pilgrims. It accommodated about fifty people, nearly all of whom during my stay were, like me, travel-travelers.

Down the length of the church's nave was a double line of open at the top cubicles and along each of the two aisles a head-to-foot line of narrow beds. Women were required to sleep single-sex in the cubicles, but in the middle of the night the sound of couples having sex echoed through the whole church.

Inside the church next to the entrance was a big table with chairs at which early every evening was an open-to-any-one poker game. In the large room tucked behind the altar was possibly world's first unisex toilet, wash, and shower room.

I lived in this church nearly a month, partly because I enjoyed the company of some of my fellow lodgers, partly because of the unlockable window in that room behind the altar that enabled me to return at any hour, and, most of all, because I more than doubled my net worth playing early evening poker. I would have stayed longer, but one night, having returned through the window, I dropped a bottle of wine on the marble floor, and its crash, louder than the sex, woke up the warden and the next morning I was kicked out.

Athens

I traveled with two young American women in their Volkswagen Bug down to southern Italy and over to Brindisi where, traveling deck class, I boarded an island-hoping ship headed for Piraeus and Athens. That evening standing alone at the railing watching Brindisi fade in the distance, someone nudged my arm. It was Allison, the lovely eighteen-year-old Californian who with me and five others had traveled in the VW bus from Madrid to Rome. For the next three nights we slept platonically next to each other on the upper deck.

The youth hostel in Athens was large, well located, and full of social interaction. At first I hung out with Allison and her cousin and the two Canadians with the van, but in the second week Liz, an African American nurse who had given me a haircut back at Toc H, turned up, and I led her up to the Acropolis and soon we were doing things together most days and evenings. It wasn't long before we discovered we had overlapping little dreams. She dreamed of traveling to Israel, and I to Egypt. We gave each other courage, and one morning we set off together hitchhiking first to Istanbul.

But that morning just before we left, Allison came looking for me in the hostel. She was sailing the next day with her cousin to a Greek island and asked me to come too. I couldn't of course, and I wouldn't mention it but, as I will explain later, knowing lovely Allison taught me something that proved important to my life.

Turkey

It took Liz and me three days to reach the Turkish border. The first night we slept in a truck cab, the second on top of a truck's load of bagged potatoes. Reaching Turkey was a relief because the Turks, unlike the Greeks, had no problems with the color of Liz's skin. The truck drivers led us to cheap hotels, and when we got to Istanbul we both fell in love with the place. We took a room in a hotel on the Asian side of the city looking down on the Bosporus. We met travelers I had met crossing Europe, did the sights, explored off the map and went up the Bosporus to the Black Sea, but the highlight was the evening two Istanbulians invited us home for dinner.

Hitchhiking in Turkey was not always easy, but Liz was a marvellous traveler, and twice we accepted invitations to stay with Turkish families. When we reached Izmir, where there was an American military base, we went into a military canteen. One table was occupied by black women, the wives of service men, and Liz went over and introduced herself. When she returned to our table, she said she had found a place for us to stay.

It was my first and only experience of being the only white in a black community. Off duty the black and white military staff and their families were totally segregated. I lost count of the number of parties we went to in our three happy days there.

THE MYSTERY OF THE TWO MARGARETS

Syria

Liz and I split up in Syria, she heading for Israel and me eventually Beirut. Syria was in a state of insurrection, soldiers with machine guns on the street corners and in trenches in the parks. In the mornings there were dead bodies in the streets. Nonetheless, daily life went on.

Bizarrely, first in Damascus and then Aleppo, I found enjoyable work that almost covered my living costs. Teenage students, all boys, were cramming for English exams, and in public parks I tutored them in small groups. They invited me into their homes for meals, and, in Aleppo, Kurdish boys forced me to play basketball with them.

Beirut

When I reached Beirut I had dysentery and belonged in a hospital. But I was in a youth hostel. Like all youth hostels, this one was closed all day, and every morning I had to beg the warden to let me stay when he locked up and left. Fortunately, he was a kind young man.

After a few days locked up in the hostel, I realized that someone besides me was frequenting the toilets. His name was Ian, mid-twenties, from England and headed for Kenya. He gave me a fat book to read, *The White Nile* by Alan Morehead. It told the stories of 19th century explorers following the Nile up to its source in Lake Victoria in Uganda. The book captivated me, and Ian accepted me as his traveling companion.

The day came when Ian and I, good health regained, checked out of the hostel, heading for our African adventure. A passenger ship with deck class for us sailed from Beirut to Port Salut in Egypt twice a week, but somehow we got its departure time wrong and missed it. The next one was not for another four days. Rather than go back to the hostel, we decided to hitchhike up into the mountains and find a place to camp. We had sleeping bags and a tiny set of cooking pots and I still had the army poncho I wore on that night walk in the rain to the youth hostel in Penzance.

On the second day, after a night on a farm family's floor, Ian and I found a small pine grove on a lower slope with a village in the near distance down below. We gathered wood for our campfire, found a spring and further down a small stream in which to wash our plates and pans. Each day when school let out down in the village, teenage boys came up to see us. They helped us with our ten words of Arabic and climbed the pine trees to fetch us pine nuts. We helped them with their promising English.

Our second attempt at catching the ferry to Port Said in Egypt was successful.

Africa

Ian's destination was Nairobi. Mine was the source of the Nile, Lake Victoria, and beyond that I didn't know where I was going. Back then, 1963, the route for the independent low-funded traveler following the Nile from Cairo to its source was like this.

- A train from Cairo to Aswan – 550 miles, 20 hours, 3rd class
- A ferry on the Nile from Aswan via Abu Simbel to Wadi Halfa in the Sudan – three days, deck class

- A train from Wadi Halfa to Khartoum – 650 miles, two days, third class
- A train from Khartoum to Kosti – 180 miles, third class
- A ferry through the Sudd, the Earth's largest swamp, to Juba – 9 days, deck class
- Hitchhiking and maybe buses to Kampala – 2 or 3 days
- Hitchhiking to Lake Victoria – 2 or 3 hours

We needed a visa for Sudan, but in Cairo its embassy refused us. The ferry had gone into the Sudd but had not come out. Until it was found, they were granting no visas to travelers passing south through their country. Every day for two weeks we went to the embassy, and still no ferry.

Eventually Ian and I decided to take a chance. We took the train to Aswan and then the ferry to Wadi Halfa, where without a visa, they let us into Sudan. In Khartoum we learned that the ferry had been found but would not be operational for at least another month. Except via that ferry, travel into the south of Sudan was prohibited, but our situation demanded an exception, and here is what the authorities arranged for us.

- 4 days on a four-wheel-drive weekly supply truck crossing the desert, then the savanna and then forest and all of it not on roads but on tracks that sometimes were invisible
- 3 days at a grass hut village waiting for the weekly train to Wau
- 4 days to Wau on a train that stopped for the night in the middle of the forest when dusk came
- 6 days on another four-wheel-drive weekly supply truck through forest and sometimes jungle to Juba

Then at the last minute, Ian secured for himself a free plane ride with England's touring football team to Nairobi, and I left for Juba without him.

My 17 days between Khartoum and Juba were the most fascinating and rewarding travel days of my life. But with one exception, they do not relate to the themes of this memoir. The exception pertains to my heritage of racism. By now, thanks to Biff, Eddy, Ted, and Liz, I was probably 90 percent cured. Late one morning near the end of my around-the-Sudd journey, a twenty-minute experience cured me completely.

We had come to a clearing in the forest with a typical village of conical shaped grass huts. Our truck stopped, and the two drivers got out and disappeared between the huts. I was sitting at the rear of the truck on top of the freight. Three young men, standing directly below me, were having a giggly conversation that was obviously focused on the extraordinarily strange man who had entered their world. Two of then wore loincloths, and the other was nude. By now, this was all an everyday sight to me. I was considering how I might interact with the three, when one of the Arab divers reappeared and motioned for me to get down and follow him into the village. After passing three or four huts we came to a surprising sight: a conical shaped, hut-sized structure of metal poles covered with metal screening. It was four days since we had left Wau, and, except for our truck and its contents, this was the first thing I had seen that appeared neither natural nor Neolithic. A tall man my age, wearing western clothes but with the same physical features as the three men who had found me so amusing, stepped out to greet me. His British-accented English sounded beautiful to my ears. He invited me into what was his home, and I sat down on a log. I already knew that I liked him, and he told me this story.

When he was two and living where we were now talking, his father was killed by a lion and his mother by an epidemic. At the time there was a young British missionary couple living in the village, and they adopted him. A year later this family of three moved to England where the son was raised British. Now, having graduated from university, he had returned for a year to his birth village to give and receive knowledge.

And so it was, that there in the flesh, in that improbable structure in what for me was the most far-off place on Earth, I found incontrovertible proof that who we are is not written into our DNA. We are all born with the ability to learn any language and to be moulded by any culture, by any set of beliefs, norms, customs, and values. Those twenty minutes deep in Africa's most remote forest was to serve me as a major reference point for the rest of my life.

A week later I reached Lake Victoria. And when a month after that I said goodbye to three young English women and a safari guide in whose large luxurious Nairobi house I had been staying, I had a new destination, the West Indies. The previous year when working briefly on a yacht in Gibraltar I had learned that every year beginning in November a few small yachts sailed from there to the West Indies, and sometimes they needed deckhands.

I went back up the Nile, this time on the ferry through the Sudd, and after stopping over in the Valley of the Kings, and Cairo and then after taking it easy for nearly a week in Alexandria, I started the three-thousand-mile hitch across the top of the continent. I did it mostly alone, and counting hospitality stopovers, it took me a month.

Yacht Dixie

I spent my first night back in Europe sleeping in an empty freight car in a railroad yard in ugly Algeciras. In the morning I caught the ferry across the bay to Gibraltar, had breakfast at Smoky Joes, then went to the public baths and then to Toc H where Jock Brown welcomed me back.

The next day Jock hired me to help him build two more bedroom shacks in the courtyard, that were only slightly less crude than my teenage clubhouse. Every morning I got up early and, before starting work, went down to the docks hoping that a yacht heading for the West Indies had come in during the night. After about three weeks one did, and I persuaded its captain to take me on as a deckhand.

That evening, I boarded what was now called Yacht Dixie. It was a two-masted, eighty-foot sailboat twice as old as me, that had been built not for oceans, but for the canals of Europe. When I boarded, it still had leeboards rather than a keel. Sailing from Italy to Gibraltar with a professional crew had been both the boat's and its new owner's first ever sea voyage. The latter, now our captain, was forty-plus with an Alabama accent and an Icelandic wife. After living for several years on a houseboat on the Thames in west London, our captain had come to think of himself as a sailor and had driven to Italy to buy this boat. Now, safe in Gibraltar's harbour, he dismissed the professional crew, and on came me and four other young men of various nationalities, one boastful of his sailing experience in San Francisco Bay. And then there was Frank, sixty-plus, who, as we were eating our first dinner together in the saloon, was introduced to us as "our navigator".

"How," I asked him, "are you going to lead us to this tiny island of Antigua on the other side of the Atlantic?"

He pointed to a small, wooded case on the floor beside the table. "With that sexton."

"Open it up and show us how it works"

"Oh God no! It's bad luck to open your sexton in port."

I felt reassured by that.

****

A week after I boarded, we crossed the Straights of Gibraltar to Africa and Ceuta to have a keel soldered on, the leeboards removed, and various leaks plugged up. Instead of coming with us, Frank went off to Seville to visit a sick friend, but when we returned to Gibraltar, he was there waiting for us. We stocked Dixie up for the voyage and were all ready to sail, but then our captain lost his nerve. Weeks passed and I had begun looking for another yacht, when one afternoon our captain came running down the dock, jumped onto Dixie's deck and said we were leaving immediately. Later I learned that back in Italy he had "forgotten" to pay for Dixie and now had spotted its former owner in Gibraltar.

Fierce currents run through the Straights of Gibraltar, and, that time of year, late afternoon was the worst possible time of day to pass through sailing west. Instead of the usual four hours, it took us nearly twenty-four to reach the Atlantic. Three days later and halfway to the Canaries, we were becalmed. Dixie had a small engine, but between the eight of us we could not figure out how to start it. After two days of trying, a breeze rescued us.

Three days later, November 22, 1963, I came on duty one minute before midnight and took over the helm. An hour later one of my off-duty mates came up from below.

"Guess what," he said. "Your president has been assassinated."

He said he had picked up the news on a Portuguese radio station in the Azores.

Two days later we reached Las Palmas de Gran Canaria and dropped anchor. We were there for a week and for no reason except the enjoyment of life. Then one evening just after dark we set sail for Antigua. The sea was rough, and I was frightened. I went below to my shared cabin and tried to sleep but couldn't. When I came on duty at midnight, the sea was still rough, the lights of Las Palmas had vanished, and I was still frightened. But by dawn the fright was gone, and, except for one near disaster, I remained like that for the rest of the voyage.

****

I soon realized that of my seven fellow voyagers, one of them, the one who informed me of Kennedy's assassination, interested me much more than the others. He called himself Dado. Beyond toddlerhood we all have two faces, the one our genes gave us and the one our life gives us. Dado, whatever the crowd, stood out, because although he was only 26, the face his life had given him already dominated the face he had inherited. Just looking at Dado made you think he had a story to tell, and the warmth and reflective intelligence in his face made you want to hear it. This gave Dado magnetism. I don't think he understood the basis of his magnetism, but he knew he possessed it, and this made him appear egotistical, and he was.

For the first ten years of his life Dado lived in a small costal town in the north of Italy. But when World War Two ended his father died and his family fell on hard times. Dado, the youngest, was sent off to live in a mountain monastery to be raised to be a priest. Dado thrived on monastery life and, although he soon became an atheist, took to the idea of becoming a priest. Occasionally the Bishop of Genoa visited the monastery looking for exceptional boys to channel towards the Church's upper echelons. When he was fourteen, Dado was transferred to live in the bishop's residence.

He liked it there even more than the monastery. But the summer Dado was fifteen, he was de-channelled. Visiting home for a month, he met on the town beach a vacationing young woman secretary from Liverpool who introduced him to sex. It was a week-long experience, after which Dado found a life of celibacy unthinkable, and, instead of returning to Genoa, he moved to Zurich, taught himself German, became a waiter and took up painting. After several years in Zurich and reaching his late teens, Dado's new ambition was to become a serious artist. Dado moved first to Paris, then to London, then the Balearics, then the Canaries, then Lisbon, and now fluent in six languages his ultimate destination was New York's Greenwich Village.

Sailing three thousand miles across the Atlantic in the trade winds is, except for emergencies, boring and undemanding. There is the occasional squall when the sails need attention, and of course the helm needs to be manned, and at dawn the dead or dying flying fish on the deck need to be thrown back into the sea. And for the first day or two your boat's slow-motion, rollercoaster ride is worrying and exciting. Sitting on deck under a blue sky I watched one huge wave after another approaching Dixie's stern, each wave as high as the masts and then lifting, lifting and lifting us slowly up into the sky. Then, but much faster, lowering us harmlessly into a deep sea-green valley. Unforgettable of course, but after a few hundred times, boring. Fortunately, back in Gibraltar, I had stocked up on novels. But, with one dramatic exception, life at sea was for me uninteresting. In the afternoons sitting on the teak deck up by the bowsprit, I compensated by engaging Dado in one-on-one conversations.

Dado had a way of looking at you after you had told him something about yourself that made you feel that he understood you better than other people did, even people who had known you for a long time. And this made you want to tell Dado still more about yourself. And people often did. Gradually Dado and I became real friends, and it was agreed that when we reached Antigua, Dado would paint touristy watercolors and I would sell them on the beaches.

****

Seven of us were below eating lunch when without warning Dixie tipped almost completely on to her side, throwing all of us into a pile on the far side of the saloon. Bruised but unhurt, each of us scrambled to the companionway and crawled up onto the deck that was now tilted at least 45 degrees. The sails were still full and moving us with speed and with the deck on the port side underwater. Instinctively we all climbed to the top of starboard and leaned back on the cable gunwale. From there, looking straight down at the water, Dixie's little keel was half exposed.

Our lives hung like that, steady-state, for at least fifteen minutes. If Dixie tipped another five degrees, then except for the drowning, our lives were over. No one, except Frank, said anything.

"We'll be okay," he said, "because I didn't open the sexton in port."

And we were. Ever so slowly Dixie's keel resubmerged, and her masts became upright. We immediately took down the big square sail hung between them and never put it up again.

****

It was all smooth sailing after that. And perfect navigation. Twenty-two days after leaving the Canaries, we sailed into Antigua's beautifully tranquil English Harbour. Frank and three of us deckhands found our way to a bar, where Frank said he had a confession to make. He hadn't really gone to Seville to visit a sick friend when we went to Ceuta; he had gone there to teach himself how to navigate and how to hold the sexton when he took it out of its case. He had long dreamed of crossing an ocean in a sailboat but knew that no one would take him on board as just a deckhand at his age.

In St. Johns, Antigua's only town, Dado and I rented an okay room, acquainted ourselves with Ros's Roost, the local's nightspot, and sourced art supplies. On Christmas Eve, I sent a telegram to my parents to confirm my continuing existence. On Christmas Day, Dado and I enjoyed dinner at the home of an Antiguan single mother who had befriended us at Ros's.

Margaret

Ultimately, we are all lonely because existentially we all live in different worlds. So most of us go looking for overlaps: "she was born in the same town as me and we both love oysters and who-done-its." But it is the overlaps that are invisible and indefinable that are the deepest because they pertain to our souls and to our existential beings rather than to our places in biology, society, and history. As I have grown older, I have grown less lonely because I have gotten better at sensing those invisible overlaps. And that morning I met Margaret on the beach in Antigua I sensed one. Not a compelling life-changing one, but one that made me think it would be good if I got to know her because maybe I could become less existentially lonely and know myself better. And I felt that maybe this woman overlapped a part of me that no one had ever overlapped before.

But initially my experience of knowing Margaret was a disappointment. An odd thing about those life-changing interpersonal interactions that we have with others, is that the time it takes for their significance to emerge varies between seconds and years. For example, that evening in the London youth hostel dining room when the Omaha beauty gave me what I saw as a meaningful smile, it right then and there gave me the beginning of a mysterious optimism that I so much needed. Ted Joan's effect on me was much slower, and our interactions spread over weeks, and although it was only days before I sensed that they were changing who I was, it was through reflection in the months and years afterwards that my knowing Ted had its biggest effect on me. Margaret's effects on me were even more delayed. Despite my optimism, my interactions with her initially not only left my existential being unchanged, they also appeared to me to have been of no potential significance. Here to begin with, I am going to relate them to you as I experienced them at the time.

****

Dado and I had not been living in Antigua long when someone told us they owned a pair of trained ponies that roamed freely, but with reins attached, on the edge of St. Johns. They said we were welcome to ride them and explained how to find them. So one morning Dado and I got up very early, found the ponies and went on our first ever bareback ride. It was open uninhabited country down to the seashore where we had the thrill of trotting through the shallows of a long sandy beach.

The next morning we did the same, and this time met a young German man living by the beach in a two-room shack. We chatted and he suggested we come there on our ponies every morning and have breakfast with him. And for a few days we did, but then I developed a problem. Barebacking was a bit much for my slender behind, and I started bleeding from my anus. Like being assigned Miss Montgomery as my American Literature teacher, my barebacking experience turned out to be one of the biggest pieces of good luck in my life.

On the morning that another pony ride became unthinkable, I decided to walk to meet Dado at the German's shack and to carry with me my big bundle of Dado's mounted watercolours, and then, after breakfast, walk the coastline to the next long beach where there were two large expensive hotels.

The walk to that beach was longer than I expected. When finally I came within sight of the Anchorage Hotel, I spotted three young women sunbathing. But because they were stretched out beyond the hotel's section of the beach, I guessed that they were not guests of the hotel and therefore not potential buyers of watercolours.

When you are old and you think back on your life and the decisions you made and that others made for you, some of the ones that have counted most may have at the time seemed utterly trivial. There have been many such decisions in my life, but one stands out above all the rest. The one I made that morning after spotting those three young women sunbathing. If I had not decided to walk over to them and have a go at chatting them up, my life would have been unrecognizable from what it turned out to be.

As I approached then, they sat up. All three appeared to be in their early to mid-twenties. One wore the scantiest bikini I had ever encountered, another a typical one and the third a modest two-piece. My attention soon became focused on the third, whose hair hung abundantly on her shoulders in curly spirals making her look Pre-Raphaelite. She was not as good looking nor as talkative as the others, and the expression in her blue eyes was oddly remote. But there was something about her face and manner that told me her intellectual grasp of life might be beyond the ordinary. She said her name was Margaret.

All three were Canadians, and all were staying at a cheap hotel on the edge of St Johns. I explained that me and the artist – I had by now shown them Dado's watercolours – were looking for another place to live.

"Ours is called Happy Acre," said Margaret ironically. "If you want you can ride back with us in our taxi and check it out." I accepted the offer, and then, since they were not leaving for a couple of hours, I continued down the beach, where I sold several watercolours.

When we arrived at Happy Acre, Margaret led me over to a little white house and introduced me to the hotel owner, an elderly woman of Portuguese descent. The hotel consisted of two, two-storey wooden buildings, one ancient and dilapidated and whose rooms were within our means. I left a deposit for two of them.

****

A few days later Dado and I moved to Happy Acre. Our building had wide covered verandas on both floors and on three sides. Our upstairs rooms shared a toilet and shower with three others. Margaret lived in the newer and much less primitive building behind ours. Below mine and Dado's rooms was a bar, popular with the locals, called Joy Land that spilled out onto the lower verandas and then onto a big terrace. When on my second Happy Acre day Margaret and I spotted each other, we sat down at a table on Joy Land's terrace and had our first one-to-one conversation. It began with her asking me the standard get-acquainted questions. Where are you from? What does your father do? Have you been to university? My answers were as boring as the questions, and then I asked her the same ones, and her answers, much longer than mine and with novelistic detail, proved unforgettable.

Her parents were immigrants from Romania, and her surname was Bezan. She had grown up on their farm in northern Ontario, which she described as "picturesque but incommodious".

"Having to venture out in the middle of the night to the outhouse is not my ideal way of life, especially in January," she explained.

But somehow at eighteen she had escaped to the University of Toronto and studied English there for two years before having to drop out because of lack of funds. Then, refusing to leave Toronto, she took a job at a "marketing research company".

"Doing what?"

"I was secretary to its manager."

Despite the past tense, I didn't ask her what she was doing now. Was she, like me, unanchored in life? Somehow it didn't feel to me that she was.

****

Several evenings a week on Joy Land's terrace, I was part of round-the-table social gatherings that were even more heterogeneous than the fireside ones back at Toc H. By now Dado had what in those days was called a "mistress", Elena. She was in her early forties, separated from her Italian husband in Venezuela, and the daughter of one of the twentieth-century's biggest opera stars, Tito Schipa. I took an immediate and lasting liking to Elena. She was living temporarily in Antigua with a woman called Carla of Capri, supposedly a former starlet of the Italian cinema. Elena was always at our table and sometimes Carla, as was the German who lived in the seaside shack, and an ex-Dixie-yacht-mate from England, the odd Antiguan, the passing traveler, and sometimes Margret and maybe one of her beach companions.

****

At these gatherings, at which Dado played the lead role, Margaret seemed more of an observer than a participant. But I found her more open when sometimes just the two of us would meet up accidently on the verandas late in the afternoon, usually each with a novel in hand. Since setting sail from Gibraltar, I had found no one to trade good books with, and by now I had even read all of Dado's James Bond novels, and I was desperate. There was only one bookshop on Antigua, closet-sized and rarely open, where among the romances I had found and bought Dostoevsky's *The Idiot*. But now I had finished it, so I suggested a trade to Margaret. Before I knew it, I was holding a slender current best-seller, *The One Hundred Dollar Misunderstanding*. It was the worst book trade of my life.

THE MYSTERY OF THE TWO MARGARETS

****

There is physical closeness and social closeness and existential closeness. With nearly all the people you meet in life, you know that however close physically you get and maybe socially as well, that existentially the two of you are not in the same world, and that it is probably impossible for it to be otherwise. But, as I hinted before, that morning I met Margaret on the beach I felt that maybe there was an overlap between our inner selves, not a large one, but for me possibly significant.

Now two weeks had passed and although we had yet to smoke dope together, in our brief conversations together at Happy Acre I had made attempts to find a point or points of existential connection. But they had all failed. So sensibly I gave up.

But then one afternoon I was a bad boy.

Margaret was a full-board resident in Happy Acre's respectable building. One of its staff told me that she and her remaining Canadian friend often never turned up to eat the lunches that were left for them on a table in the dining room. Feeding myself was a problem, not so much because of money, but because the nearest affordable restaurant was a long walk away. One afternoon when it had gone three and an ex-yacht-mate of mine was visiting and we were both starving, I led us across to the respectable building and into its deserted dining room where on a white tablecloth two lunches were waiting for us.

We were half-finished when Margaret appeared and froze in the dining room's doorway, then turned and disappeared. I leaped up and ran after her shouting apologies and begging her to stop, but she ran up the stairs. I started to run up after her. She reached the landing, turned, and disappeared and started up the next flight.

"Please let me walk you into town and buy you lunch."

Suddenly the situation felt strange. We had both stopped moving. I couldn't see her; she couldn't see me. We were standing on different levels and by now she knew I wasn't going to come up the last three steps and around the corner, but – and this is what was strange – now I felt closer, a lot closer, to her than I ever had before. There was even a tinge of intimacy in the long silence before she answered.

"No, it's okay. I'm not really hungry. Don't worry about it. It's no big deal."

There was another silence, and I said sorry again and turned around and walked back down.

****

I thought I had probably just imagined it. I mean thinking that the eating-her-lunch episode had cut down the distance between Margaret and me. Two days passed, and I hadn't set eyes on her and I was now caught in that dead time when the afternoon has finished and it feels like the evening will never begin. I was alone in Joy Land sitting on a stool at the bar with a drink in my hand. A car pulled into the drive. A taxi. Margaret got out. She took three steps, spotted me and changed direction. She came over, stepped into the bar, and sat down on the stool next to me and started talking to me like we were old friends. Except she asked questions that old friends wouldn't need to ask. Like, "How old are you?"

"24."

"I'm 24 too. What month were you born in?"

"March."

"Then you're much older than me. I was born in November."

We laughed and she accepted my offer of a drink. There were some more biographical exchanges before our conversation got on to books. I was saying something boring about one of Jean-Paul Sartre's novels when she interrupted me.

"Someday if you get the chance, you should read *The Second Sex*, by Simone de Beauvoir."

I knew of Beauvoir as "Sartre's mistress", and I went straight back to talking about Sartre. Nonetheless, like Miss Montgomery giving me a two grade for imagination, Margaret enunciating for me those three words, *The Second Sex*, was to prove one of the most important gifts of my life.

****

At the far end of that long beach on which I met Margaret was Antigua's most expensive hotel, the Caribbean Beach Club. It had a bar out on the beach to which its guests seemed more attracted than the sea. Reclining on pink sun-loungers, they usually waved me away when I offered to show them Dado's watercolours. One day in the white sand behind a lady's sun-lounger I saw jewels sparkling. It was a bracelet, sapphires probably, but maybe diamonds. I stepped around to the front of the lady's lounger and dangled it.

"Is this yours?" I asked.

"Yes, it is," she said as she grabbed it. No thank you, no eye contact.

I told Margaret this story a couple of nights later sitting at the bar in Joy Land. When I finished she said, "Your marketing is all wrong. But maybe I could help you."

She was going to the beach tomorrow, and we could share a taxi there and back, and she would show me a different sales technique. Of course, I accepted.

When we left the taxi, Margaret told me to wait fifteen minutes before coming down to the beach of the Caribbean Beach Club.

I found Margaret reclined in one of the sun-loungers near the bar.

"Excuse me. May I show you some watercolours?"

"You'd be wasting your time," she answered in a loud voice."

"Please have just a quick look."

"Well OK, but five minutes max."

Again Margaret had spoken in what for her was an unnaturally loud voice, and as I opened my portfolio I noticed that other sunbathers were looking our way. When I held up the second watercolour, she rudely grabbed it, gazed at it for what seemed a long time, and then laid it in her lap.

"Next."

I held up another and again she grabbed it and put it in her lap. And then another.

"Maybe," she said. "Next."

THE MYSTERY OF THE TWO MARGARETS

By now two of the sunbathers had risen and were standing behind Margaret's chair and soon there were more. It continued like that for maybe twenty minutes, at the end of which Margaret had "bought" two and I had sold six.

****

A few days later sitting at a table on the upper veranda, I was mounting Dado's watercolours when Margaret spotted me and came up. I put down my knife, and we started chatting.

Beyond toddlerhood we all have two sets of facial expressions, those that emerge spontaneously from within and those calculated to convey a meaning to observers. Heretofore it was only the latter, with rare and fleeting exceptions, that Margaret had given me. But now sitting opposite me on the veranda her face was mostly unguarded, and this encouraged me to be more personal, more explorative.

Initially I had presumed that she went to the beach – Antigua claimed 365 of them – every day, but by now I realized that she spent most of every day in her room in the other building. Why? The longer I knew Margaret the more of a mystery I found her. And I had yet to observe anything secretarial about her.

"What do you do all day in your room?" I asked.

"I scribble."

"Scribble what?"

"Oh, school-girl poetry mostly."

I can't remember what I then said, nor exactly what I thought, but I accepted her description. And I can still see the uncalculated expressions on Margaret's face in the minute or two that followed – the way she moved from slight hope to expected disappointment. But at that point in my life, I was blind to what was happening, blind to the cause and meaning of Margaret's expressions. Because I had been raised as a sexist, like every male of my generation, it did not spontaneously enter my mind that Margaret might be "scribbling" in her room all day because she was trying to master the art of writing. My everyday sensibilities may have been half-free of sexism, but not my intellect, not the categories that without thinking I applied to life. With Dado when I learned of his artist aspirations, I immediately encouraged him to think beyond tourist watercolours. But that afternoon on the veranda, it never occurred to me in encourage Margaret in the same way. And unknown to me, I lost not only the chance to become better, maybe much better, friends with Margaret, but also to give her a small but personal gift.

****

For the next week or more Margaret seemed to be avoiding me, and this made me reflect and to question my negative presumptions. I even reclassified her in my mind as possibly a serious would-be writer of some kind and hinted to her that I had done so. She continued to ignore me.

Then late one afternoon I was lying on my bed half asleep when there was a knock on my door. I got up and opened it, and there was Marg, as I now called her, in her modest two-piece swimsuit.

"Did I wake you up?"

"Almost."

She looked a little nervous.

"Can you come out and play?" she asked with a deadpan smile.

I sensed she had come with something special to tell me. I stepped out and followed her to a corner of the veranda, where leaning against the railing, she at first looked away from me and out at the tops of the palm trees. Then she turned around and raised her eyes toward mine.

"I was wondering if you might like to go with me to Half Moon Bay tomorrow. My old boss from the firm I told you about is staying with his wife at the Half Moon Bay Hotel and has invited me there to lunch. But I don't really want to sit through a whole lunch with them, so . . . . "

Her idea was that in the morning we could walk to the harbour in St Johns and buy a lobster from a fishing boat, bring it back to Happy Acre and boil it somehow, and then take a taxi, which she would pay for, to Half Moon Bay on the far side of the island, have a swim, eat the lobster, and then walk to the hotel and have desert with her ex-boss and his wife.

Of course, I agreed.

****

We bought one of the three live lobsters squirming in the bottom of the fisherman's little boat. Neither he nor us had anything to carry it in, so I had to carry it by gripping the back of its neck all the way back to Happy Acre. There awaiting us was a bucket of boiling water on a charcoal grill. When Margaret saw that I was having difficulty dropping the now highly animated creature into the boiling water, she told me to put it on the ground. I did and she immediately picked it up and dropped into the bucket. When the taxi arrived, I was moderately disappointed to learn that one of Margaret's beach companions was coming with us.

Half Moon Bay is on Antigua's windward side where the surf can be forbidding. But across the mouth of Half Moon Bay is a red coral reef over which the surf breaks and then tints the beaches pink with bits of coral. When we arrived, the long pink beach on the left side of the deep-blue bay was completely deserted. We went for a swim, ate the lobster, soaked up the natural beauty, and then walked to the hotel on the other side of the bay, where Margaret's ex-boss and his wife were finishing their lunch on a shaded terrace. We spent a pleasantly boring hour with them, but as I will explain later, it was an hour that as the years passed increasingly haunted me.

****

I think it was a couple of days later that Margaret moved out of Happy Acre's respectable building and into the one I lived in. It was now February, the hotels were filling up again and their rates increasing, in this case apparently beyond Margaret's means.

One morning before I had left for the beaches with Dado's watercolours, Margaret knocked on my door. She was wearing her blue two-piece swimsuit. She said she wanted me to do something to her hair and led me into the washroom that we now shared. She said her long and somewhat curly hair periodically needed the special treatment that I was about to give it. I can't remember the exact procedure, but she lowered her head into one of the two brown basins – I think partially filled with water – and from a brown bottle I poured a smelly liquid and then for maybe five minutes churned her hair in the concoction.

I remembered this tiny episode because at the time I thought that what she asked me to do was something that one would ask someone of the opposite sex to do only if they thought of them as a friend.

****

I had spent the evening at Carla of Capri's house with her, Dado and Elena; and when I arrived back at Happy Acre and turned on the light to my room, I saw on the floor what looked like a note someone had slid under the door

I'm returning to Toronto tomorrow. My taxi is coming at 11:00. I thought maybe we could meet below for a goodbye coffee at about 10:30.
Margaret

I turned up before 10:30 and so did she with her suitcase. I felt disappointment as we sat down. Not because she was leaving, but because I had failed to find that overlap I had sensed that morning we met. Today, however, it was immediately apparent that there was something different about our rapport from what it had been at the wash basin and on the beach at Half Moon Bay. There was more formality in our manner towards each other than even on the day we met, and yet our conversation was more directly personal than it had ever been. I think we both soon became aware of the contradiction, as we sat there in the shade on the lower veranda, Margaret's lovely hands laid flat, palms down, on our table.

"What do you plan to do with your life when you get back to the States?" she asked.

"I don't know. First, I must figure out who I am. I mean on the inside. I don't understand myself. So I'm going to get books on psychology and psychoanalysis, maybe Freud, and psychoanalyse myself."

"I tried that. It got me nowhere. It was a waste of my life"

The way she was talking to me now gave me a strange feeling. It was almost as if she saw me as a separate person from myself, as if I were someone other than who I was.

"I have to try."

"You shouldn't. Really. It's a waste of time."

"I don't know what else to do."

"Well, I'll tell you what I did. I didn't understand myself either, but after wasting my time trying, I decided I would just plunge ahead with life and figure out and create myself as I went along."

"No, I've promised myself that first I must figure out who I am."

Of course, after half a century I can't remember exactly our words that morning at Happy Acre, but I think that the dialogue you have just read is true to both its spirit and content.

"Well maybe we can meet up in ten years and see whose strategy worked best." (Those were Margaret's exact words.)

"Yes, maybe we can. And you, are you going to pursue a career as a writer?"

"Oh God, no. I had more than enough poverty when growing up. I'm going to look for a better paying job. Maybe even a rich husband."

Then – ten minutes early – her taxi arrived.

"Goodbye", "Goodbye", nothing more.

I watched the taxi drive away. I wanted to call it back. I wanted to ask Margaret questions about who I was. This was the ultimate irony, but it would be seventeen years before I would fully see it.

****

Dado was extremely conversational, and I had many conversations with him on all kinds of topics. But the one that proved the most important for me came near the end of our knowing each other and not long after Margaret left. The time was approaching when I would be returning to my broken roots in the States, and Dado had begun to take an interest in my future. One morning on the veranda outside his room, he said, "You have a big decision to make, probably the biggest decision you will make in your whole life."

"What's that?"

"You have to decide who you are."

"What do you mean?"

"I mean you have to decide whether to return to being the person you were before your travels or to continue with the reinvention of yourself. And that won't be easy. It may be easy here, but it won't be when you return to your homeland. And if you do decide to reinvent yourself it may bring you happiness in the long run, but I think it will be a long hard struggle. You have to decide."

I had nothing to say in response, because I had never thought of my life that way. But immediately I could see the truth and wisdom of Dado's thoughts about me, and I filed them away with Margaret's parting thoughts. But making the choice Dado had described was more difficult than even I realized, because I still did not really know who I was.

****

I left Antigua on the deck of an island-hopping freighter, and after a few days disembarked at Kingston, Jamaica and booked into its YMCA. A few evenings later, I met up with Dado and Elena. They were staying at a hotel that had been a favourite of Errol Flynn. When at the end of our long luxurious evening together at their hotel it came time to say goodbye, I guessed – and it turned out to be true – that I would never see either Dado or Elena again. So, for me it was a sad goodbye. It was also very late and too dangerous to walk back to the YMCA, so I spent the night on a deck chair in a back corner of the hotel's huge high-walled garden

Me searching for me

The Second Sex

There in Jamaica, for the second time in my two years of traveling, I boarded a plane, and flew to Miami where I soon noticed that the instinctive awkwardness between me and young women was as strong as when I left. I was horrified. How could this be? And when I thought about it, I became more horrified because I could find no explanation as to why this radical retransformation had come about. It couldn't be a question of nationality, because most of the many young women whose company I had effortlessly enjoyed from Isles of Scilly onwards had been Americans and Canadians. I tried not to think about it and told myself that it would pass, that it was just part of the shock of being back in my home country.

THE MYSTERY OF THE TWO MARGARETS

My parents had moved to a retirement village in Southern California. First, I bused up to Washington DC to visit my Aunt Helen and her husband, and then, with stopovers in Chicago and Lincoln, hitchhiked three thousand miles to Los Angeles where in the smog I found my parents' "village" tucked between roaring freeways.

My mother was glad to see me, my father not, and neither appeared to notice any change in me nor, unlike Helen, show any interest in my experiences. It was as if the me of the last two years had never really existed. Then two weeks after I arrived, my father fell ill. Two or three weeks later he died. His final words to me, followed by his last laugh, were "You'll never be of any use to anyone."

****

After a trip back to Nebraska for the funeral and burial, and a few weeks helping my mother adjust to her changed life, I moved up to San Francisco. I had decided, mindful of Dado's thoughts but without ever really thinking it through, to go back to being, with adornments, the person I had been raised to be. I would find myself a career job, and after a few months I was offered one in an insurance company.

I turned it down. When I stopped to think about it, I couldn't see myself sitting year after year in its windowless offices reading insurance policies. I switched my job-hunting to banking. I started reading the *Wall Street Journal* and books on high finance. Wells Fargo, which like now was one of the world's ten largest banks, had its skyscraper home office on San Francisco's Montgomery Street. I went halfway up it for an interview. It wasn't for any job in particular, but the personnel man soon got the idea that I might make a good financial analyst. The investment department was looking for a trainee, and after two more interviews they offered me the post. The investment department's offices were the plushest offices I had ever seen, and becoming a financial analyst almost appealed to me. I accepted and was scheduled to start in nine days when my trainer would return from his annual vacation.

Two days later I had a radical life-changing moment. I was sitting on a stool eating a bowl of chilli. I was at a U-shaped lunch-counter a block off Union Square. In the aisle to my right was one of those revolvable wire book racks. I couldn't read the titles from where I was sitting, but I could see that most covers featured pictures of shapely young women with torn blouses and hiked skirts. Mostly Mickey Spillane whodunits I figured. Then I spotted a cover with a photograph of a completely nude woman. I promised myself that I would stop and have a look when I finished my chilli and was on my way to pay my bill.

It was soft-focus, but she really was nude and for some reason the book was enormously thick. Eventually I read the title, The Second Sex. Margaret's words rang out in my mind, "Sometime you should read The Second Sex by Simone de Beauvoir."

The 700-page small-print book of great seriousness was being marketed with the leud murder mysteries because, as I explained at the beginning of this book, Mrs Knopf of Alfred A. Knopf Inc. on a trip to Paris bought the English rights for what she thought was a sex manual. When the Knopfs learned that it was not a sex manual, they decided to go ahead and package it as if it were, a decision for which I am enormously grateful.

My retransformation back into a young man who was seriously ill at ease and inept with young women had not relented. And though I tried to find one, I had no idea about why it had happened nor how I might return myself to the young man whom I had so much enjoyed being for a year and a half. But I wasn't thinking about that when I paid for my bowl of chili and the book with the lewd cover.

I took *The Second Sex* back to my Nob Hill bedsit and started reading it. And when I did, I couldn't stop. For the next four days I kept reading it and thinking about what it told me *about me and my life*. The situation appeared to me utterly preposterous. There I was reading a book by a French woman and learning more about my individual manhood than I had ever dreamed of knowing. I don't think the term "sexist" even existed then, but the word "bigot" did and within a day of being seduced by the book's cover I realized that, like nearly all my contemporaries and our parents, I was a common variety of bigot.

When I finished reading *The Second Sex* I was not yet a feminist – that would take a few months of reflection – but I knew I wanted a life that included lots of companionship with women like I had enjoyed on my travels, and within twenty-four hours Beauvoir's book had answered what had become the biggest unknown in my life: why I didn't get on with most women my age but with a few very well, all of whom I found when I was traveling. Why when traveling?

Because back in the early Sixties the only young women who would have wanted and dared to go traveling on their own were privately (there was not yet an equal rights, equal opportunities movement) in rebellion against their society and its culture. And it was no accident that so disproportionately many of them were nurses, they having matured in a profession led by women. But why were these young women and I predisposed to each other? This required thought.

Unknown to me, as Ed-in-the-neighbourhood, I had for ten years transgressed social norms regarding relations between the sexes. From five to fifteen-and-a-half, I, despite my obsession with sports, had regularly enjoyed one-on-one companionship and equal-to-equal friendships with numerous girls. For all those years my closest friends were evenly divided between the sexes. And then there was Aunt Helen. Like her friend Tanya, she was a product of feminism's first wave back in the twenties, and when I was growing up and coming of age, Helen, between assignments, often came to stay with us. From an early age, of all the adults I knew it was Helen's company that I most enjoyed and that became my ideal.

This background of my neighbourhood friendships and my Aunt Helen predisposed me, despite my thoughtless acceptance of my society's norms and beliefs, to immediately engage with young women as my existential equals, which most found off-putting, but a tiny few seducing. It was unlikely that I would ever meet any of the latter at Wells Fargo where it was plain to see that it was corporate policy to deny women full human rights. Women worked there vis-à-vis men only in radically subservient positions. Even their facial expressions, I had noticed, displayed constant deference to their rulers. None of the young women whose company I had enjoyed on my travels could have survived in that milieu without degenerating. Without knowing it, for nearly two years I had enjoyed the company and sometimes the intimacy of young women who believed in their right to Liberty and Equality and who were silently engaged in self-emancipation. What would having a career at Wells Fargo mean for me and my relations with women?

I was due at nine o'clock for my first day with Wells Fargo. Dressed in my brown suit and red tie, I caught a cable-car to the bottom of Nob Hill and Montgomery Street. It was only quarter to nine when I came to the Wells Fargo building. Reaching the door, I decided to stroll for a few minutes before going in. When at five-to-nine I came back to this entrance to my future, I couldn't make myself go in. When it got to be ten-thirty and I had strolled up and down Montgomery Street half a dozen times, I gave up opening that door.

Who am I?

I first heard of San Francisco's City Lights when visiting Ted Joans in Tangier. It was one of Ted's publishers, and I hadn't been in San Francisco more than a few days when I visited its paperback bookstore in bohemian North Beach. It was on multiple floors, and I soon made its basement my second home. Some of Ted's books were down there and it was brightly lit and there were large round tables with chairs, and I sat there four or five nights a week reading for free, sometimes till near midnight. I never bought anything, and no-one ever bothered me.

Around the corner from City Lights was a bar like nothing I had ever seen before. It was called Vesuvio, and although it became the place in San Francisco I most wanted to go in, I was afraid to go in. Every time I left City Lights on my way back to my bedsit at the top of Knob Hill, I walked past Vesuvio and slowed down and some nights I even stopped. Unlike other bars, Vesuvio had big clear plate-glass windows and I could see the hanging tiffany lampshades inside, the red velvet upholstery, the dark wood tables and the upmarket bohemian crowd. It was that crowd that for me was both the main attraction and what made Nebraska-me afraid to enter. I had never seen upmarket bohemians before. I imagined that they were worldly successful artists and writers and their agents and hanger-ons. I still hadn't gone in to Vesuvio when a couple of months after my early morning walk up and down Montgomery Street and with my-thousand-dollar inheritance from my father mostly gone, I moved across the bay to Berkeley and found work as a dishwasher.

****

The sixties were less than a year old when I moved to Berkeley. The Vietnam War was raging but the Peace Movement was beginning to emerge, and it was now my wish to become part of it. But first I had that prior commitment to fulfil for myself. In Antigua when Margaret and I had our farewell conversation and we disagreed about how best to handle our psychological irregularities, I was sincere when I said I intended to explore my inner self with the guidance of psychology and psychiatry, and now was my chance.

Because – and as I suppose it was also like this for Margaret – my character and sensibilities had not been formed in conventional ways, the general culture did not offer me as much insight into my inner self as it did for most folks. Most of the people I knew were less of a mystery to me than I was to myself. This narrative you are reading gives a false impression of what it felt like to be *me* back in my early youth. I am writing it from the perspective of an additional half-century of life, so I can't help but make my early adult self appear more understandable than it was when I was living it. The truth is that my self-knowledge and self-understanding back then was, with few exceptions, significantly less than that of my peers.

The university's huge library was only a fifteen-minute walk from my new bedsit, and it granted me a library card. Soon I was reading Freud, Adler and Jung, and then their disciples and offshoots. Increasingly, except for washing dishes, I did little else. Months of this passed and I was becoming a hermit. But none the wiser. Maybe even dumber and more confused and, for sure, more than a little depressed. But then reading Sartre's *Being and Nothingness*, a philosophical work, its long Part Three: Being-For-Others gave me a couple of ideas about who I was and who I could become and soon I was reconsidering Margaret's strategy and advice. And then I adopted it; I plunged back into the world like I was. Except for Sartre's, I never looked at any of those books again.

But initially my plunge from solitude back into full life didn't go well. It was almost a plunge into nothingness. The world had ceased to smile for me: no romance, no interesting encounters, no intriguing new ideas, and no success at gaining entry into the inner circle of the New Left.

As always, I was skinny. By some process of reasoning, I decided that if I could overcome this defect, then the world would smile for me. So one morning I walked down to Berkeley's sleepy main-street, entered a health food store, and left with an enormous can labelled Mussel-On. Soon I was over-eating three times a day and sluggish around the clock but gaining weight. On Euclid Street was a drug store with a scale outside its door. Every Monday I got up on the scale, inserted a penny and out popped a tiny card with my weight printed on it. After ten weeks I had gone through six of those giant Mussel-On cans and gained thirty-four pounds.

A few days later my fortune changed. I found my way into a Berkeley soiree. It met informally every Friday evening in someone's house and was frequented by graduate students, professors, New Left activists, Haight-Ashbury artists, rock musicians, visiting pilgrims from the interior, and all of them, except the undercover agents, were for their time subversives of some kind. From that first Friday, once again, like that night I drove the retired ice cream van from London to Dover, my life took off. My in-the-world existence took over from my thoughts about why I was like I was. And I was fully aware that now I was following Margaret's advice when one evening I dumped my psychology books into an empty drawer. I even forgot about how much I weighed. One morning three months into my new existence I was passing the drugstore on Euclid when I remembered its scales. I walked over and dropped in a penny. Of the 34 pounds I had gained, I'd lost 32.

I never worried about my weight again.

****

There was one episode in my Berkeley life that relates in an ambiguous way to the larger story I am telling you. Remember Allison? That good-looking adventurous eighteen-year-old that I met in Gibraltar and then by accident in Madrid and then traveled with to Rome and then met by accident again on the deck of a ship headed for Greece. Well, this time it was in Berkeley. I had been leafletting and it was starting to rain, and I took shelter in the Student Union where I sat down with the *San Francisco Chronicle* in a row of armchairs facing another row and started reading. When twenty minutes later I accidentally bumped the feet of the person sitting opposite me, I lowered my paper and there was Allison. Both of us placed a hand on the other's knee to make sure they were real.

And it was just like before, only more so. Here was, in my categorical eyes, the perfect young woman, and she *was* a woman now and available, but like before our individualities – those foes of corporate life and formula fiction – wouldn't connect. There was no magic between us. We saw each other a few times, films, coffee-house dinners, and a peace march and that was it. But through the decades lovely Allison has frequently popped up in my memory.

****

The Friday evening soirees opened doors for me, and by late '65 I was deeply involved in The Peace Movement and on the steering committee of what was said to be then America's largest New Left organization. My traveling days were now submerged in what seemed a distant past. I was no longer, or so I thought, on a journey to discover myself. I had rediscovered half of me and enjoyed the illusion that that half was all of me. With one exception, all those generous nobodies who had helped me substantiate that half no longer existed for me except as vivid phantoms.

THE MYSTERY OF THE TWO MARGARETS

The exception was one of my cross-Atlantic yacht-mates, an Englishman, who turned up at my door with his girlfriend one midnight. They were living in San Francisco's newly created Haight-Ashbury, the birthplace of the counter-cultural movement that, when it came to the enjoyment of sex and the use of language, included equal rights for women. Soon I was leading a double life: Berkeley political activist Monday to Thursday and Haight-Ashbury counterculturist Friday to Sunday. And so it pleasurably continued. But in the spring of '68 *Time Magazine* convinced me that Bobby Kennedy, who was running as a peace candidate, was destined to be elected the next President, and therefore I decided my Berkeley activism was no longer needed.

****

It was now the summer of '68. Although I was living in the Haight, most evenings I hung out in North Beach, circulating between flats, studios, galleries, and bars. If it is possible to be a voyeur to one's own life, then at this point in mine I was one. I allowed myself to be flattered by the company I was keeping, mostly artists with growing reputations who to my amazement and delight sometimes in the evenings – and I think this is what turned me into a self-voyeur – led me to Vesuvio. So now I was almost one of those people I had envied.

Late that summer an especially attractive young woman with a suitcase full of mini dresses moved in with me. She was a recent escapee from Oklahoma but possessed a degree of street cool that I have seldom seen matched. One evening with her on my arm – neither of us was significantly attached to the other – I for the first time *self-entered* Vesuvio. We took a table under a tiffany lamp, facing the door. Twice, pairs of regulars entered who knew me and came over to our table. Perhaps not so much to say hello to me as to see close-up my companion. They were impressed, and this should have been my moment of triumph: I, Nebraska-me, had made it in the Vesuvio world. But when the second pair of admirers left our table, my triumph collapsed. Not because of worldly happenings, but because of something that happened in my mind: the realization that I had taken the wrong path.

Despite all my idealizing, like everyone else the main thing I was seeking in life was happiness. For me this required, among other things, self-respect. Somehow seeing the displays of admiration by the visitors to our table, made me realize that, despite what others now thought, I didn't think as well of myself these days as I had the year before and maybe before that and I was becoming less happy the more that worldly success became mine. So how then might I achieve my main goal in life?

Within hours I came to feel desperate. Maybe at fifty I could give up on my dream of steady-state happiness, but not at twenty-nine.

So the great longing of my now unquiet heart was once again to have belief in a dream that said I was on the road to happiness. What is most important about dreams is not them coming true – sometimes after the first hour they can become boring – but in believing that they will. My Vesuvio moment had made me realize that I had dreamt a false dream: that worldly success would not bring me happiness. But how would I find a dream to replace it? It was time again for deep fantasy, and I indulged. Every day I took a long walk in Golden Gate Park, and it was one windy afternoon up on Strawberry Hill that a crazy new dream took hold of me: *If I can find the right life-time partner, happiness will be mine and hers also.*

But then I asked myself: What kind of a person should I be looking for? Ahh, but that's the wrong question, I realized. Knowing Allison has taught me that. It's not a kind of person that I need to find, I shouldn't be looking for someone like Allison, someone who matches a checklist of ideals. Instead, I must look for someone whose uniqueness intersects in a binding way with my own uniqueness.

Of course it was an unfounded dream. Maybe no such person for me had ever existed. Thinking back over the women, and there were more than a few, whom I had known rather well since living in California, I couldn't think of any whom I could have thought of as a possible candidate. This reflection proved a serious downer and threatened my still teetering new dream. Only serious and immediate action would save it.

But how?

On the road again

I decided I needed to break with my San Francisco and Berkeley life if I were going to fully redirect my energies to my new strategy for finding happiness. So a few weeks after my Visuvio moment, I and another troubled male soul loaded a VW van with Haight-Ashbury psychedelic posters and headed east aiming for poster shops in university towns. A few months later we reached New York City and Greenwich Village where I spent a couple of mostly miserable deep-winter months. Then I drove back west a thousand miles to Madison, Wisconsin.

On my slow cross-country trip I had spent two weeks in Madison and had become well-acquainted with several of its co-eds and enamoured with its wooded lake-side campus. It called itself the Berkeley of the Midwest, which I thought was a bit sad, but among its 35,000 students and 12,000 teachers I thought there was a chance that I would find a person who would make my happiness dream come true.

But a year-and-a-half passed, and I was still looking for a life-partner. Most of the previous year I had been living with a woman whom I had considered a possibility forty miles west of Madison at Taliesin, the architect Frank Lloyd Wright's estate. In June 1970 I moved alone back to Madison, found temporary lodging near the Student Union, made new friends with two co-eds, and started hanging out at their much-visited two-storey apartment. They shared it with a third girl, Katie, who they said was engaged and lived mostly with her fiancé. Without ever setting eyes on her, I became curious about her. In one of the bedrooms there were two mattresses and two bookcases, and one of the latter captured my interest. It was Katie's, they said. When I commented on the sophistication of her reading, they said she had never been out of Wisconsin. But what really kept me wondering about the unseen nineteen-year-old was that one of her books was a well-thumbed copy of *The Second Sex*.

Late one evening I had gone up to that double bedroom to escape a crowd of people downstairs. I was sitting alone with a book on one of the mattresses, when a young woman entered carrying a guitar case. We mumbled hellos.

She sat down on the other mattress, got out her guitar and started strumming.

"Are you Katie?" I asked.

"Yes. Are you Edward?"

I don't remember how our conversation then took off, but it did. And it wasn't long before I directed it toward *The Second Sex*. I suppose because I wanted her to know that I too was a fan. We had only been talking for about ten minutes when I thought OH MY GOD, maybe I have found her. And I panicked. Literally. I stood up, left the bedroom and went downstairs. I needed to think for a few minutes about what I should do. But should I do anything? By now I was accustomed to having good-looking women friends. Katie wasn't homely, but neither was she what you would call good-looking. And she had just told me that come Sunday afternoon – it was now Thursday and nearing midnight – she was moving for the summer to a different city. That, and given that she was engaged, made it the longest of long shots. "But what the hell, I'm going to give it a try".

Katie was still on her mattress playing her guitar. I sat down on the other mattress and when I asked her about her studies, she stopped strumming. She said her ambition in life was to be a high school English teacher. I told her, with complete sincerity, that that was too modest, that she should aim to become an English academic. She said that that was unrealistic, and then – her speaking voice was mysteriously beautiful – she told me a few things about her family. Its extreme humbleness made me think of Ted Joans and Margaret Bezan. Here are the opening paragraphs of Katie's 2003 obituary in *The Guardian*.

The American-born Kate Fullbrook, who has died at 52 from breast cancer, was an eccentric and outspoken English don, who, for two decades, campaigned forcefully on behalf of Britain's new universities and the value of a liberal education for all. She wrote several influential books and, at the time of her death, was associate dean for research and staff development in humanities, languages and social sciences at the University of the West of England (UWE), in Bristol.

Born in Sheboygan, Wisconsin, Kate was the daughter of an arc-welder whose formal education had ended at the age of 11. Her parents dreamed of better things for their three children, but none the less opposed her university application. So, on the night of her high school graduation, she went into hiding for the summer, and enrolled at the University of Wisconsin, in Madison, that autumn.

It was 1968, and Madison was a focal point of the social and political questioning then unsettling Nixon's America. For Kate, it was a wonderful new world; she earned top marks, was elected to Phi Beta Kappa, played in an all-women rock band and graduated with the highest honours.

Then came a shattering blow to her self-confidence. The university English department put her name up as their first choice for a federal research studentship but, a month later, she was told that her profile did not fit the requirements of the scholarships, probably because of her association with anti-Vietnam [War] activists, notably Edward Fullbrook, whom she married in 1972.

Part II: Margaret Atwood

Margaret's ghost in the Lost Valley

I am, you realize, telling you a story whose links are more than just chronological. And for me, although some will say it is an illusion, my impressions in life, past and present, are linked neither by deep Cartesian structures nor by Hume's superficial bundles, but by narratives, some of which were inculcated in me as part of my upbringing, some of which I have encountered and engaged with as an adult, and some, like the one you are reading, which I have made up. And proudly so. My life, like Ted's, Margaret's and Katie's, has been a struggle to create for myself a story other than the one that fate and society assigned me. A struggle that continues but that of course now lacks the life-and-death urgency it still had for me 50 years ago. Back then the superstructure of me that is me now was still only partially formed. Edward-the-retarded was only two-thirds dead, and in the winds of life the new partially formed Edward often wobbled. I was painfully aware that the self-created me needed strengthening and I looked for ways to do so.

I was now thirty-three years old, and it had been eighteen years since I had extended Ed-in-the-neighborhood's fantasy of mental normality to my whole life. It was 1973 and Katie and I were living in Spain on the Costa del Sol in a small town called Nerja, which back then had more fishing boats pulled up on its sandy beaches than tourists. I had been right about both needing a life-partner and choosing Katie. Happiness and self-respect now seemed almost natural dimensions of my daily life.

But real life is never without problems. And sometimes the biggest problem is that you don't understand your problems. When at 22 I became intellectual, it was my belief in my *pretend* level of intelligence that was fortified. And more and more every year. The intensity and regularity of the pleasure that my intellect gave me, freed me from having to give time and energy to maintaining my fantasy of normality, of believing I had not deserved to be taken to the school basement every week. But it changed nothing in terms of the fundamentals of my two self-identities themselves. It did however gradually change the relation between the two. Because intellectual pursuits and reflection increasingly dominated my life, awareness of what for me was my "real" self dropped more and more into my unconscious. Clinically, I was becoming more neurotic than ever, and it repeatedly manifested itself in one situation. The more intellectual I became the more often I had thoughts or combinations of thoughts that at least in part were my own. But to hold a pen over a blank sheet of paper with nothing to copy or respond to, like an examination question or someone's letter, filled me with panic. One tablet of paper would have in those circumstances lasted me three lifetimes.

For you to understand my writer's block and the private mental event that was to happen to me in the Lost Valley, I think I need to try to explain better how I was constructed as a psychological entity. Though now in my thirties, my weekly existence was a mostly unconscious war between two sets of stories. There were the stories that when I was growing up adult society told me about who I was and that now, although pushed into the background, echoed day and night in my mind. And there were the stories I had created and repeatedly told myself about who I was. If in my last year of high school I had had a different father and if the school authorities had formally taken me aside and told me that they had made a big mistake about who I was and apologized, then, with some strong counselling, the war that Ed-in-the-neighborhood had started could have been ended within a year or two, with Ed-in-the-neighborhood its undisputed winner.

The war could also have been mostly ended in a very different way. If that morning on Montgomery Street in San Francisco I had managed to open that Wells Fargo door, I would have had by now, 1973, not only my private stories to substantiate my intellectual adequacy, but also my years of ladder-climbing with its daily suit-and-tie status. My other me would still have been there, but, like the ground hog, would have only infrequently and inconsequentially showed itself above ground.

But instead, I had lived a life not only without institutional support and definition, but also one that did not fit into any well-defined social or cultural narrative. My positive self was grounded on the stories I had created and told to myself. One of the most strategic of those stories was the one I have told you that begins with that late afternoon conversation with Margaret up at the bar at Happy Acre. It was only because of her private and thoughtful words to me that I came to understand my relations and proclivities with women. As storytelling goes it was a good story: young woman tells young man he should read a book by a French woman, which later he does but only because of its lewd cover, but nonetheless the book gives him an understanding of both himself and his culture deeper than he had dreamed of having and completely changes the direction of his life. But I never told this story to others, only to myself. It not only described in me a deep structure but also one that by now was substantiated by an abundance of worldly evidence. So for a long time I treasured this story for its, or so I had thought, indisputable reality. But as time passed, this story as it lived in my mind developed a reality problem: Margaret Bezan. No longer seeing her in the shadows of the moment, thinking about her now was increasingly like waking up in bed in the morning with someone who except for their body you don't really know.

****

Supposedly I was now living there in the isolated Spanish town to write a book, but my writer's block had another four years to run. Even so it was mostly good times for Katie and me there in Nerja; and one day, I, all alone sitting in a meadow at the top of an uninhabited no-road mountain valley, "reencountered" Margaret Bezan.

Oddly, my Aunt Helen played a part in bringing this about. She was retired now and a widow and lived half the year on the Costa de Sol near Marbella where she enjoyed the fellowship of a small circle of other retired spies from various counties. Katie and I exchanged visits with Helen several times, and once when visiting us she told us a story that she had drawn from a local taxi driver.

There was once what was now called the Old Granada Fish Trail. It was a trail on which in centuries past fish were transported by donkey up to Granada. A few miles above Nerja was a village called Frigiliana from which according to the taxi driver you could pick up the fish trail and walk over the first mountain ridge and into what was now called the Lost Valley. Something terrible had happened there after General Franco had come to power in the 1930s. Near the top of the valley and beyond all roads there was a hamlet inhabited by Spaniards opposed to the fascist dictatorship and who engaged in secret resistance. Eventually the village was discovered, its inhabitants killed, and their houses destroyed.

To old Ed-in-the-neighborhood, Helen's story immediately suggested an outing. Especially if someone would come with me. Katie wasn't interested, but there was a tiny expat community in Nerja in whose headquarters – an English-language second-hand bookshop in someone's living-room – I had become acquainted with a young UK academic on sabbatical living in Frigiliana with his wife and small child. When a few days later I suggested the walk to him and his visiting friend, they jumped at the idea.

We set off from Frigiliana early in the morning. It was one of those Mediterranean winter days when the sun shines and you can walk in your shirt sleeves. The three of us, the only visible non-locals, walked through the car-free twisted lanes and with help from the locals found the path that would take us up over the ridge and into the Lost Valley.

Up at the summit, the trail worn deep by centuries of loaded donkeys, passed through a gap in the rocks, and suddenly we came out into what seemed like another world. A deep narrow valley. Down below us, our side was forested. Opposite us, up at the top of the other side, was a small steeply terraced vineyard where we could see a man, the only real person we would see in the valley, tending the vines.

An hour later we reached the hamlet. It looked as though once it had been a dream hamlet. Eight or nine destroyed little houses on the bank of a gurgling stream. An arched stone footbridge and an olive grove on the other side.

My companions wanted to walk further in the valley, but for reasons I did not yet understand, I wanted to stay there near the dead hamlet. It was agreed they would walk further in the valley and return in an hour and a half.

Just beyond the ruined houses a meadow ran up the slope. A tiny construction near the bottom caught my eye, and I walked over. It, I guessed, was a shepherd's shelter, chest high and made from grass and small branches. It remined me of the "forts" I had built as a child in the field overlooking the Rock Island train tracks. I sat down on its open side and gazed down at the dead hamlet. Sitting there on the grass in that beautiful, haunted place, it felt like there was only me and this place in the world. But I didn't want to think about the place's story. Instead, I got to thinking about one of the stories I told myself to cover up my identity with my retarded past.

I have been using the word "stories", but maybe I should say memories or recollections. One usually recalls memories without converting them to words. But like paragraphs, memories are edited. As you recall memories, you reshape and reorganize them to better illuminate your changing life. Surely everyone does it. I did and doing so was one of the primary means by which I became the person I am. And that day sitting alone in the Lost Valley I did some major memory reshaping.

As time had passed, my going to university and being a graduate student lost their narrative pull, and increasingly the memories I used to hide my other self came from post-Nebraska happenings: rediscovery of my natural means of connecting with the opposite sex, Ted Joans teaching me to identify myself from the inside out, and Margaret pointing me towards *The Second Sex* and to a strategy, that at the time I rejected, for getting on with my life. Yes, my story of who I now was depended especially on those two gifts I had been given at Happy Acre.

Most weeks Margaret's two gifts along with Miss Montgomery's gift of a red star, and Ted's leading me to invert the foundation of my identity, and now Katie giving me a day-by-day happy life, supported the fantasy I had begun with Ed-in-the-neighbourhood. But increasingly there was for me a problem with the reality of Margaret. It came partly from learning from my own struggle of breaking free from my inherited destiny and partly from witnessing Katie's struggle to do the same. There were things I knew or thought I knew about Margaret that for me, like a weak character in a novel, no longer added up. Had she really existed?

Every young person is potentially capable of redefining and remaking themselves when they leave home. But it comes about not by magic, but by hard work, mistakes, embarrassments, the passage of time. And no matter how much time passes, there are limits to how far the new creation can go. Especially if one does not plug into a social or cultural movement of the time.

Ted Joans had escaped from the prison of racism by taking on a loud public identity, a beatnik, that *proudly* proclaimed his differences from his prison guards. Katie's existential escape from the wrong side of the tracks was still only partial – and, as I would discover, more partial than I had thought – but it had been greatly assisted by her inclusion and identification with the counterculture that was then a key player in the evolution of her country's culture. But Margaret, except when she pointed me toward Beauvoir [it was before the launch of the second wave of feminism] and when she dropped the live lobster into the pot, had displayed no signs and given no hints of any socio-cultural deviance from white big-city middle-class. As she told her story, her transformation from her agrarian outhouse existence with immigrant East European parents had been engineered without social help like Ted and Katie had had, and yet six years later she had displayed to me no traces of her social-cultural origins. And there was another loose peg. Had she really been just the secretary she claimed to have been?

That day Margaret took me with her to meet her ex-boss at Half Moon Bay I came close to asking her that question.

For an hour I had watched and listened to her and him and his wife in conversation. He didn't talk to Margaret as someone who had been his personal secretary, and then at the end he said he very much hoped she would come back to her old job. But surely by now he would have hired a new personal secretary.

Leaving Half Moon Bay that day, we teamed up with other people to share a taxi back to St Johns. There were not enough seats, but Margaret said that was okay; she would sit on my lap. We hadn't gone far when I found myself thinking I should ask her about what her real job at the market advertising research firm had been. But then I realized that with Margaret sitting on my lap and my thinking about her, I was beginning to get an erection. So immediately I switched to thinking about President Kennedy's assassination.

It was not until after I had read *The Second Sex* that Margaret became important enough for me to think again about that Half Moon Bay episode. And it was when I did, that I began to wonder how much of the story she had told me of who she was, was fiction.

It was my living with Katie that really destroyed my belief in Margaret Bezan. Katie was now only two years younger than Margaret was in Antigua, and yet it would be many years before and maybe never that, like Margaret, she could present herself to the world as a middleclass thoroughbred.

I suppose it was the combination of the private humiliation I was experiencing now living in Spain as I tried to write and my now sitting there on the edge of a hamlet that no longer really existed, that motivated me to rethink the memories that I used to substantiate my self-identity. I had previously considered dumping Margaret from my memory chest, and now gazing down at the destroyed hamlet, I decided to go through with it.

Revising my stories was easy. Henceforth my discovery of *The Second Sex* would begin with my attraction to its lewd cover, and the strategy of making myself up as I went would be credited to my reading *Being and Nothingness*. Sitting there by the shepherd's shelter I made a promise to myself. I would no longer deliberately think of Margaret Bezan.

I kept that promise for eight years and seven months.

Escape – stage three

Identity problems

I have made it sound easier than it was. Even today I can find myself in a state of panic because of something that was or wasn't said to me that makes me think that I really am mentally retarded. But it is only a ghost and so passes quickly and at worst causes only momentary humiliation because deep down I know that I am not. But I was 37 before that deep-down belief became mine. It was born in tears one morning sitting alone in an armchair following the third of three good luck experiences that through the kindness of others befell me in a period of eight months.

The first came in the summer of '76. On the surface I was completely healed from my bad experiences with the school system and my father's sustained efforts to make them everlasting. By now I was well-read, intellectually conversable and I even had a larger than average vocabulary. But although for most of two decades I had ambitions to write, I never succeeded in putting my own words onto paper even when I made myself sit down off by my lonesome. Whenever I tried, I panicked. I did not understand why. Inside I was someone else and I didn't know who. Existentially I was still two Edwards. Edward-the-retarded had not died, he had just gone underground, and deeper and deeper as my life passed. But he came roaring to the surface whenever I faced a blank sheet of paper in a room alone. Creatively, I was still in that windowless basement room at Sheridan School.

Katie also had an identity problem that stood between her and her dreams. It was visible to me that night we met in her bedroom, but it was not until four years later at a dinner party that I realized just how deep it was.

We were living in Madison again, when a middle-aged couple with whom I had socialized the year I lived on Frank Lloyd Wright's Taliesin invited us for dinner at their lavishly converted barn near Wright's estate. Our host ran an advertising agency in Chicago, and our hostess directed a local theatre group that performed in a Wright-designed theatre. The only other guests were a young couple who were close friends of Katie's and mine.

I think it proved to be a lovely evening for everyone except Katie. As her obituary hints, she was a lively talker and unusually witty, but on this evening, she said nothing. Why, I asked myself? Because, I answered, our hosts were straight middle-aged middleclass. I had seen this social paralysis take hold of Katie before when in the company of her former professors and their wives, but I had failed to appreciate its seriousness because I attributed it to academic deference. Now I realized that the range of people with whom she was unable to be herself was very much broader than I had thought. Furthermore, this inability had to be psychologically deep, because in four-and-a-half years I had seen no signs that it was diminishing. But a story she had recently told me helped me understand it. The story was an example of the class humiliation Katie experienced when growing up, especially as she approached adulthood.

When she was fifteen there was a long strike at the factory where her father worked. When she was told to find work to help put food on the family table, she found work as a mother's helper for a family with a daughter in her year at high school. One day the mother sent Katie to the grocery store to buy a lettuce. She returned with a cabbage. That story, Katie said, was told and retold around town many times, especially at her high school.

By now Katie had decided she was ready to enrol at our expense as a graduate student there in Madison, but after that dinner I came up with a crazy idea. If the straight middleclass people she dealt with were British rather than American, they would probably not trigger her phobia because for her their Britishness would swamp their middle-classness. I went to the university library and did some research. I found two British universities that offered Master's degrees that fitted Katie's needs. One was Queen Mary's College of the University of London. Not only did Katie need a new platform to launch herself from, but also Ed-in-the neighbourhood needed some adventure. After a couple of weeks, Katie was persuaded.

I did some more research. I wanted to find out if any of Queen Mary's English faculty had connections with

Oxbridge where Katie might do her PhD. They did. One had until recently been a tenured member of the English faculty at Cambridge University. I checked him out and found him to be a Henry James specialist. On her application form, Katie said she wanted to do her Master's thesis on Henry James.

When in the autumn of '75 Katie and I moved to London, the Henry James specialist became Katie's tutor. He had left Cambridge to marry a professional bridge player who was a Guinness, one of Britain's wealthiest families. They lived in The Albany, a hidden apartment complex off Piccadilly next to the Royal Academy. The Albany has appeared in numerous novels, including ones by Dickens, Oscar Wilde, P.G. Wodehouse, Ian Fleming, and Graham Green. It has also housed dozens of real-life quasi-immortals, and now once a week Katie went to The Albany for her tutorial. After six or seven weeks we were invited there for a small dinner party, at which Katie was vigorously verbal and totally Katie.

****

We hadn't been in London a month, living in a horrid ninth floor studio flat in remote Woolwich, when we realized that our funding was seriously insufficient. I found a church near the Ritz Hotel and the hidden entrance to The Albany where I could make brass rubbings. I started sending them to a bookstore back in Madison. It sold a few, but I knew sales would stop come Christmas. But maybe I could sell them to the tourists there in London. Every Saturday and Sunday along Piccadilly over a hundred artists and crafties hung their creations on Green Park's railing. One Saturday

I screwed up my courage and went down there at dawn and captured three feet of railing. Although thousands of tourists moseyed by, in eight hours I sold nothing. But the middle-aged cockney next to me and with only 18 inches of railing made what for him and me was more than a good day's earnings. He even made the crap he sold as he sat there on the pavement. Horseshoe nail jewelry he called it. Horseshoe nails bent with round-nosed pliers into funny shapes, then bound together with fuse wire (I had to ask him about that) and then hung on a fake silver chain.

In the back streets of the East End I found a metalworks that sold horseshoe nails, in Camden a hardware shop that sold the funny pliers, in Covent Garden an electrician's shop that sold the fuse wire, and in Soho a junk jewelry wholesaler who sold the chains by the hundred. It then took me a couple of shut-in high-rise Woolwich weeks, with the BBC World Service giving me moral support, to reach a degree of craftmanship that enabled marketing.

There were already three people hawking the nails at Green Park on Saturdays and I was sure I would meet active resistance if I tried to become the fourth. But there was only one on Sundays, and not the cockney, and one week I went down there, claimed a pitch at the far end and came home with more cash than I had hoped. And so it continued.

Can't-Remember-His-Name

But then at the beginning of the new year, an extraordinary piece of good luck upped our living costs. We moved into a big-windowed one-bedroom Georgian flat overlooking a Bloomsbury garden square. Now living within easy walking distance of all the temptations of central London, our horseshoe nail income no longer sufficed. So I found a job working four nights a week as a bartender. Bartending in London was the beginning of the full death of Edward-the-retarded.

The summer of '76 was the hottest English summer on record, and I loved it. I made and hawked the hideous jewelry, played tennis on the court in our square, and went to theatre matinées where I would buy a ticket for the Gods and then just before the curtain went up help myself to a seat in the empty front row. And four nights a week I bartended in a private bar on Mecklenburgh Square where we lived. The bar had no street entrance and was the size of someone's living room, but with a high ornate ceiling, two crystal chandeliers and walls covered with red velvet and life-sized gold-framed oil portraits of pompous old men. My actual bar – the one I tended behind – was tucked into a corner with four stools in front of it. Most of my customers were foreign graduate students and professors on sabbatical, and every evening they packed the room between six and seven before heading to the far side of the square for dinner. In the quiet hour that followed, I made the bartender in Humphrey Bogart's *Casablanca* my conversational model: I would find out what my customer's obsession was and then feign fascination.

There was the thirty-something Canadian behavioural psychologist who wanted to be told she was sexually attractive; there was the macho Australian marketing professor who wanted us to talk about how horrible French wine was compared to Australian wine; and there was the customer who I enjoyed by far the most and to whom I now owe so much, but whose name, and I regret this deeply, is lost to me. I will call him "Can't-Remember-His-Name". He was an American in his late twenties and near to finishing his doctorate in the philosophy of science. The philosophy world tends to lumber through twenty-year infatuations, and in the seventies, it was with the philosophy of science; and London, where its superstar Karl Popper and leading adversaries were based, was its Mecca.

As a topic of conversation, I preferred epistemology to the horribleness of French wines, but with one exception my knowledge of the former did not extend beyond the 19th century. The exception came about back in my Berkeley days after I had escaped from self-analysis and had taken up Margaret's advice and as a peace activist my life had taken off again. One Berkeley day, for now forgotten reasons, I decided to familiarize myself with logical positivism, then still the 20th century's dominant school of epistemology. I checked out one of its key works from the university library. This turned out to be a bad experience that ten years later, thanks to Can't-Remember-His-Name, transformed my life.

Back in Berkeley I gave that book my best, but after two days of trying to see light, I gave up. I can still see, and still with disgust, the slender blue hardback lying there. But I didn't have so much arrogance as to be able to say I was right and the positivists were wrong about science and verification, so I dropped completely both the subject and my bad experience from my thoughts. And if I hadn't become a London bartender ten years later, they might never have returned. But life is so weird, so different from what the psych books tell you. You have some little experience that turns out bad, like mine with that book, and you forget all about it, and then one day it does you a big favour. In this case an enormous one. One that, thanks to Can't-Remember-His-Name, changed me on the inside, one that enabled me to write this and other books.

There was nothing memorable about Can't-Remember-His-Name's physical presence, except the strong sincerity in his face and voice. But he had a conversational obsession, the philosophy of science, especially Karl Popper whom I had never read. When I learned that Popper was opposed to logical positivism, my conversational engagement with Can't-Remember-His-Name soon transcended my bartender's role. And soon most evenings at about seven he sat down at my bar.

Two weeks of these discussions had passed when one evening he introduced a twist. He said every Friday morning he and four other PhD candidates met in the office of Nicholas Maxwell, a philosophy of science lecturer at University College, for an informal three-hour seminar, and that I should join them. Of course I declined, and likewise the next week, and then he gave up. Or so I thought.

It was early Friday morning, and someone was knocking on our door. I was still in bed, but Katie was up, and she opened the door. A man who was a stranger to her explained that he had come to take me to the seminar which he described. It was the first Katie had heard about it, and now Can't-Remember-His-Name had an ally, because Katie thought it was a splendid idea. I'm a bit weak-willed when I first get up, and they both went to work on me and within minutes I was being led across Bloomsbury to University College.

On the walk I decided I would say nothing in the seminar, absolutely nothing. I was greeted by the others, especially by Nicholas Maxwell, with extreme scepticism.

Clearly, they all thought that Can't-Remember-His-Name had committed a no-no.

But that made it easier for me to keep quiet, and for an hour-and-a-half I did so effortlessly. But then, to my horror, I heard my voice. I had become so interested in what was being said that I had forgotten my vow. I tried to stop, but they insisted I continue. Soon the whole group was engaged in discussion in a way they hadn't been before, and we ran past the three-hour mark.

When over lunch Maxwell invited me to come every week, the others voiced their approval. And I did until the end of the summer term.

You can probably see the significance of that for me. It wasn't as magical as my Miss Montgomery red-star moment, but being so gratuitous and unsolicited, it made me begin to take my intellectuality with more self-sustained seriousness than I had previously. There on that Bloomsbury square it was a summer in heaven for me, and between horseshoe-nail bending and bartending I read most of Popper and then numerous others writing about the philosophy of science.

****

Last year, beginning at Paddington Station, I strolled across London, through Hyde Park, down Oxford Street, into and across Bloomsbury and down the hidden pedestrian way behind Coram's Fields that led me into Mecklenburgh Square where I stopped to gaze at Goodenough House. It was in its hidden bar at the back where 46 years ago Can't-Remember-His-Name enhanced my fantasy of writing books. Today I think of my bartending as the beginning of my CV.

My evening with a somebody

In the autumn of '76 we moved to Cambridge UK so that Katie could pursue the PhD she had been stopped from pursuing four years earlier. Back in my Berkeley days, once I had taken Margaret's advice and stumbled back out into the world, most days I socialized and sometimes worked with graduate students and faculty. Generally, the academic world, like the aristocracy, is in its everyday existence finely tuned to rank. This social norm inhibits academia's serious everyday conversations, because rather than speaking, listening and thinking freely one tends to defer to the person perceived to be the topic's authority. But among Berkeley academics I found a shared sense of intellectual equality that, if I wanted it, included me. In time I came to realize that paradoxically this equality was born out of a kind of arrogance. They saw Berkeley, along with a couple of other places in the world, as the intellectuals' heaven of heavens, which for them meant that whatever your certification and bibliography, your being there conversing with them in Berkeley, meant that you, like them, deserved to be heard.

But this indulgence came with a price, because if you said something stupid or insufficiently informed, as I sometimes did, rather than being politely overlooked or gently corrected, you were immediately attacked. Yet overall, those Berkeley conversations offered me a degree of respect that, except sometimes on my travels, I had never known; and of course they boosted my confidence.

Madison's academic community, however, had lacked the arrogance needed to give me the same. But there was no shortage of that arrogance around my Bloomsbury and Cambridge, so beginning at the bar in Mecklenburg Square and now socializing in Cambridge, my intellectual self-worth was again, like in Berkeley, receiving weekly boosts. And this despite the fact that in Cambridge I was working as a decorator, transporting myself and my tools on an ancient postman's bicycle.

We hadn't been in Cambridge long when one afternoon walking on a backstreet near the city market I found myself gazing into a shop window. It was a photographer's shop belonging to the widow of Frank Ramsey, a philosopher, mathematician, and economist who back in the 1920s died famous at the age of 26. The shop window was full of old black-and-white photos, and soon I was recognizing faces from the Bloomsbury Group: Virginia and Leonard Woolf, Duncan Grant, Keynes and others. One photograph was larger than all the others and the longer I stood there, although I didn't recognize the subject, the more I found myself looking at it: a woman in her early to mid-twenties in an oddly patterned dress sitting on a sofa with her legs folded under her. It wasn't that she was particularly good-looking but rather that there was more character in her face than you would expect in someone her age. Eventually I leaned down to read the small print on the bottom of the frame: "Joan Robinson". She was, you may remember, the author of a book explaining Keynes' *The General Theory*, that agreed with my own reading but went much deeper.

There was a dimension to my experience with that Joan Robinson book that I thought best to wait until now to tell you. Back then (1961), like nearly everyone else, I was a hardcore sexist. So much so that initially, although previously I knew "Joan" only as a woman's name, I assumed this Joan was a man and credited this usage to British eccentricity. But soon the graduate student who had loaned me the book assured me that Joan Robinson was a woman. I hate the word "amazing" but I really did find this fact amazing. (I'm telling you all this because it is a good example of how bigotry can work silently and undercover.) Then I noticed that the book's title page identified Joan Robinson as a "Reader" at Cambridge University. I had never heard of such a title, but neither had I ever heard of or even imagined a woman teaching economics, so I assumed that she was just an extremely strange case who was associated with Cambridge in some loose and unique way and had been given this title. Nonetheless, I read the book a second time, and Joan Robinson, after Keynes, became my second intellectual hero.

A few nights after gazing at the photograph of Joan Robinson in her youth, Katie and I were at a chamber music concert. It had yet to begin, and I was watching people taking their seats. An elderly couple, entering arm-in-arm, caught my eye. The woman sitting next to me appeared to recognize them, so I asked her who they were. "They're famous economists: Piero Sraffa and Joan Robinson."

A month later at a dinner party I found myself sitting opposite an Indian woman who was a Cambridge English don. Her name was Sita, and I soon learned that she had grown up in Delhi and that her father had been high up in India's foreign office, and that when she was a teenager, she had frequently accompanied her father to diplomatic cocktail parties. I calculated that that must have been in the late 1940s when my Aunt Helen was stationed in India.

"Did you perhaps ever meet someone at those functions by the name of Helen Gilmore?" I asked.

"Helen Gilmore! How do you know her?"

"She's my aunt."

"She was one of my favorite people. She was so much fun to talk to. My father thought maybe she was a spy."

I now had Sita's full attention, and we mostly talked literature until we got to the cheese course when she asked what I "read" in university. "Oh", she replied, "I too did a degree in economics. After my undergraduate degree in English, I decided to get one in economics before going on for my doctorate in English." She said she kept up her economics contacts and occasionally had "econ evenings" and she would invite me to the next one.

I had zero interest in economics, but when a few weeks later I received the promised invitation, I thought it might be interesting as a social occasion. So, more than a little nervous, I went along.

I was the last to arrive. Entering a large sitting room, I found that there, in an armchair directly in front of me, was Joan Robinson. The gathering had been forewarned that an odd American was coming, and I had barely crossed the threshold when the great woman, with the whole room listening, asked me a question about the current state of the American economy. She did so with the kindest possible face, but I had not read anything about any economy for over a decade, and I froze. Thankfully, Sita covered for me, and dinner was served.

After dinner – by now I had had a couple of glasses – I decided I had to make something of this once-in-a-lifetime opportunity to engage with one of my heroes. Joan – there was absolutely no edge to the woman, so it already seemed natural to think of her as Joan – was in the armchair again, and I sat down on the floor facing her at her feet. I began by asking her what it was like being a student at Cambridge back in the twenties. After recalling the lectures of the literary critic I.A. Richards, she moved on to Wittgenstein and Sraffa and their weekly one-on-one discussions over tea. It was one of those discussions – and in her raspy voice she repeated Sraffa's account of it – that led to Wittgenstein's famous turn from belief in a world comprised of atomistic sets of propositional facts to one where meaning depends on the anthropological setting in which propositions are conveyed. At this point Sita, who was now sitting on the floor beside me, sought to bring the whole room into the conversation by making a broad and potentially contentious statement about the meaning of Wittgenstein's *Tractatus*. I still had not read the book, but had read one or more books about it, and, suspecting it was likewise with Sita, I decided as a way of becoming friends with her to argue against her. It was immediately obvious that she liked my challenge and soon the whole room of economists was debating the meaning of *Tractatus Logico-Philosophicus*. And, bizarrely, something was about to happen that would change again the course of my life.

As the debate continued it occurred to me that perhaps no one in the room had really read the *Tractatus*. Joan Robinson stayed out of the debate and, although I was still sitting at her feet, I now had my back to her. Then suddenly from behind me her loud raspy voice broke into the conversation. Here are her exact words.

"The world is all that is the case. The world is the totality of facts, not of things. The world is determined by the facts, and by their being all the facts. For the totality of facts determines what is the case, and also whatever is not the case. Those are the first four propositions of the *Tractatus*. I've never been able to understand them."

With her eyes turned away from us and into her thoughts, she tried to explain what she couldn't understand. She was not arguing; she was making a confession. Except for maybe herself, the singularity of her behavior was lost on no one in the room. It was a magic moment for me – the relaxed integrity of her intellect was so plain to see. And it was such a direct contrast to the outcome of the conversation I had had sixteen years before with the professor and graduate students in Nebraska. That night when I got on my postman's bike and pedaled home, I felt like something very strange was happening to my mind.

Gift of a book

After my evening with the economists at Sita's, I checked out a few economics books from the city library. I told myself I was doing it to help me conversationally when people asked me what I "read" in university and who then would begin conversing with me as if I were an economist. Katie noticed these books and interpreted it to mean that I was thinking of reengaging with economics. She knew that Keynes along with Sartre was my number-one intellectual hero, and that it was my reading *The General Theory* that had turned me into the intellectual whom she had married.

That first year in Cambridge we were seriously poor, sometimes going without dinner, and with Christmas approaching we agreed we would give each other only one inexpensive present. On Christmas morning, I was therefore horrified when I opened Katie's present and found myself holding *The General Theory*. As I told you earlier, one day as a graduate student back in Nebraska I had gone to a professor I much respected to show him a page in *The General Theory* that I believed contained a small argument that was logically flawed, but that was in no way strategically connected to the rest of the book. But the professor had quickly declared, without explaining, that it was me who was mistaken, not Keynes. This might have been an inconsequential event if it had not happened the same week as when my father implied that I lacked the intelligence needed to do a PhD. It was the combination of these two events that had sent me into psychological meltdown. Since then, except once accidentally, I had never again opened *The General Theory* until now, with Katie watching, and me reading her inscription: "With hopes that this will provide you with many days of absorbing interest."

I thumbed the book, pretending to browse, and thanked Katie profusely and sincerely, because although it was the worst possible Christmas present for me, I saw the deeply thoughtful goodwill behind it.

We were now about ten days into the new year. It was mid-morning, Katie had gone off to her college, and I, between jobs, was stuck at home in our humble flat. I was sitting in an armchair with **that book** lying on the lamp table next to me. I had yet to read a single word of it. But now I began to ask myself: Why was I afraid of it? And **suddenly the answer popped into my mind**; and for the first time as an adult, I began to cry. I was afraid to open it because deep-down I still believed that I belonged in that basement room at Sheridan School. "But I don't. Really! I'm not faking it. **REALLY, REALLY**," I screamed.

Off and on for the next three-and-a-half-hours I cried, partly out of grief for the decades lost, and partly out of the joy of knowing that I would, when given the time, be able to write.

****

Meanwhile, there were walls to paint and nails to bend. Cambridge had a large arts-and-crafts community whose biggest source of livelihood was a summer market in All Saints Gardens, a tiny triangular city park opposite the gate to Trinity, Cambridge's richest college. I didn't have a place in the market, but I had acquaintances who did, so when word got out that the city council, under pressure from Trinity, was going to end this market, I put my Ed-in-the-Neighborhood skills to work. In a few weeks I created the Cambridge Arts and Crafts Association with nearly a hundred members, and after two visits by its representatives to the city council offices the cancellation plan was dropped.

Come summer, me and my horseshoe nail jewelry were given space at the market. At the end of the following summer, I was sad that Katie and I were leaving Cambridge.

Margaret's ghost in the Black Mountains

These days the standard track to becoming a novelist is not that different from becoming an accountant. One goes to university, the more highly ranked the better, and studies "Creative Writing", and then with this formal technical training one goes out into the world looking for something to write "creatively" about.

But there was a time not so long ago, when the road to becoming a novelist, at least a serious one, usually ran in the opposite direction. Because one possessed a strong set of individual sensibilities and maybe some stories that went with them, one sought the technical skills by which to express them in fiction. It was substance that begged technique, rather than the other way around.

I needed to say this here at the beginning of this chapter because the story upon which it turns presumes belief in the deeply individual sensibilities of great novelists.

****

Katie's memory was quirky. For twenty years she watched "Top of the Pops" every week and ever after could remember the lyrics to nearly every song. She also remembered every detail of every story she had ever heard me tell, which sometimes proved annoying. But when it came to remembering what *she* had said about this or that, she remembered almost nothing. And it was this shortcoming of Katie's that led me to a second encounter with Margaret's ghost.

In autumn '79, we moved to Devon where Katie took up work as an English lecturer and I set about becoming a writer and once again an economist. We lived in a charmless house on the edge of Dartmoor, a mostly treeless 300 square miles of rocky hills inhabited only by sheep and wild ponies. The open moor was only a five-minute walk away, my tennis club eight, and after we acquired a Siberian husky puppy, I spent an hour walking on the moor nearly every day.

In the two years that followed I became so obsessed with economics and epistemology that, for the first time since my evening on the couch with Aunt Helen and Hemmingway, I stopped reading fiction. I didn't want this to continue forever. That's why when one evening over dinner Katie mentioned a novelist who was celebrated in his lifetime but now forgotten, I asked her what contemporary novelists she thought would still be read a century on.

As I expected, she liked this question, gave it some thought and then gave me three names. I wrote them down, and then after dinner stuck the list of three at the back of one of my desk drawers.

A few months later Katie and I were talking great books again, this time sitting atop Pew Tor, when I thought to ask her my great novelists question again. As before, I wrote down her three answers, and then back home blindly stuck this list in the drawer with the other.

More months passed, and I still had not found time to read any fiction. But we were about to go on holiday for a week in Wales in the Black Mountains and I was determined that then and there I would read a novel. Which one? I remembered Katie's two lists, and now for a third time I asked her to nominate three living potential literary greats. As before, I jotted down the names, but this time I went up to my study and got out Katie's previous answers and compared the three sets. In total there were seven names, six on only one list and one on all three. Katie had recently reviewed the on-all-three author's latest novel, and her review copy went with me to the Black Mountains

We had rented an isolated cottage with two friends from Cambridge and their two small daughters. On our second evening, when everyone disappeared into the sitting room, I stayed in the kitchen with a pint of scrumpy and the novel by the living author for whom Katie predicted immortality. I read for two hours.

That night, sleep-wise, was the strangest of my life. During the day we had walked up and down the "mountains" and when I went to bed, I went straight to sleep. Two hours later I was awakened by the most vivid dream I have ever had. Vivid in the sense that it felt like it was really happening to me. But, paradoxically, not much happened in the dream and it lasted only a couple of minutes. It was the intensity of the dream, more real than real, that had put me, now awake, in a state of shock. What was happening to my mind that caused me to have this dream unlike any I had ever had? There was no way I could now go back to sleep.

Without waking Katie, I got out of bed, found my way downstairs to the sitting room and turned-on lights.

My dream had gone like this. I was in Philadelphia at a large economics conference. I was about to enter a full auditorium where I was to give the keynote paper. Several journalists holding reporters' notebooks were standing at the entrance. One stepped forward to speak to me, and it was Margaret Bezan. "Good luck," she said.

She was wearing a loud-patterned, hot-colored dress, mostly green and blue but with flashes of orange and yellow.

"This isn't the tropics," I said. "You shouldn't be wearing this dress." And it was at that point that I woke up.

Now, sitting wrapped in a blanket in the unfamiliar room with three lamps lit, I tried to make sense of my dream. Why Philadelphia? I asked. I had never been to Philadelphia, and had no desire to go, and knew nothing about it. Ahh, but I did know one thing. It is called "the city of brotherly love". And that explained it because, except for that moment in the taxi, my relationship with Margaret had been entirely platonic. And yet, especially after San Francisco and Berkeley but before I had encountered her ghost in Span in the Lost Valley, I had felt a gratitude towards her that could have been called love.

But why in the dream was I now about to enter an auditorium to deliver an economics paper? That too was easy. The belief that came to me on the day of my big cry in Cambridge had turned out to be correct. Since relocating on the edge of Dartmoor, my research and writing had gone well, even better than I had hoped, and I now believed that the day, although still a long way off, would come when my economics work would gain recognition.

But why Margaret Bezan? Why should she be the star of my dream? That also was easy to answer. Back in Antigua she had given me those two thoughtful nudges that subsequently had catapulted me to where I was now.

But why tonight? And here in the Black Mountains of all places. This once in a lifetime dream. Why? And why was she holding a notebook? And why the dress? Why the big deal about her dress? And why did I wake up then?

Unable to answer these questions, I was driven to do something foolish. Since the age of sixteen I had been a pack-a-day smoker. Beginning at about thirty I had made attempts to break the habit, and now for the first time I was near to succeeding. For six weeks I had been smoking, a few puffs at a time, only one cigarette a day. But the next hour and a half, for the first time in my life, I literally chain-smoked. When seven cigarettes later I snuck back to bed, I still had no clues to the answers to those questions.

Come morning, I was the last up. The bathroom was downstairs and to reach it you had to go through the kitchen. The others were sitting at the big table eating breakfast. As I said good morning, I glimpsed from the corner of my eye a familiar flash of color. I turned to see it full on and saw the pattern and colors of Margaret's dress in my dream. It was the dust jacket of the novel I had been reading before I went to bed. By the time I reached the bathroom I couldn't help but half believe that the novel I had been reading, *Bodily Harm* by Margaret Atwood, had been written by my Margaret Bezan.

****

Before I can continue with this episode, I need to make a short detour.

If it had not been for something that happened to me the summer we lived in London, it would have been natural for me that morning in the Black Mountains when leaving the bathroom and sitting down at the kitchen table with Katie and our good friends to have told them the story that I have just now told you. But I didn't because of something that happened to me the year we lived in London. On those hot summer nights when at eleven I closed my bar, I frequently dragged customers back to our flat for more drinks and conversation. One of my favorites, and a weekly opponent on the tennis court, was a young American graduate student, David Manasian. On this particular night there were four or five of us, and it was past midnight and I had been blabbering on about something when David said, "You like to namedrop, don't you?"

I was horrified, because David's words made me realize that just then I had namedropped and that it wasn't the first time and that maybe it had become a habit. Namedropping was feasible for me, because when living in sixties Berkeley and San Francisco, some of the people I mixed with were or became household names. I was privately ashamed of myself; and, thinking about it the next day, I made one of my resolutions: I will never namedrop again.

****

When we returned from the Black Mountains to Devon, I had still not told Katie about my dream. I suppose because the only explanation I could offer for my dream was that the two Margarets were really one, and on a worldly or objective level my explanation looked extremely improbable. The only correlation between the two that the book's dust jacket provided was that they were both Canadians and had the same first name. These days it would be simple to see if there were a further correlation just by doing some Googling. But back in the Eighties, one still needed to go to the library. A week after our return I ventured into Plymouth and its city library.

I expected the one-Margaret hypothesis to be quickly and decisively falsified. First, I found several black-and-white photographs of Margaret Atwood, and although they were consistent with how I remembered her, they were inconclusive. But then I found some reference books giving biographical details of living authors of fiction and poetry, and here is what I learned:

- Margaret Atwood was born in Canada in November 1939.
- Margaret Atwood studied English at the University of Toronto in the late 1950s.
- Margaret Atwood worked for a market research firm in Toronto in 1963.

These details corresponded perfectly with details that Margaret Bezan had given me about herself.

Now with knowledge of these correspondences, I found myself thinking on my daily Dartmoor walks of more profound correspondences:

- Margaret Bezan had a passion for reading serious fiction, and surely Margaret Atwood did also.
- Margaret Bezan spent most days writing for long hours, and obviously Margaret Atwood did also.
- Margaret Bezan, given that she urged me to read *The Second Sex*, was a feminist before the word was widely known, and from what I had surmised in the library, so also was Margaret Atwood.

I set my hands on all the novels Margaret Atwood had published. There were five. Katie owned four. I read *Lady Oracle* and then *Surfacing*, and *Surfacing* left me feeling elated for days. Not because of its story but because I thought and still do that it is one of the deepest novels I have ever read. I reread Chapters 10 and 15 every decade.

****

The summer following our holiday in the Black Mountains, Katie and I stayed in Cambridge for a week with friends, and Saturday afternoon on a grass tennis court, Margaret's ghost reappeared. With a tennis racket I had walked over to the tennis club where I had played when we lived in Cambridge. I was welcomed back, and in my second set my doubles partner, who was new to me, introduced herself as Eleanor. "Eleanor", I said to myself. "I used to know someone named Eleanor. Who?" Midway through the set it came to me.

It had been an Antigua Happy-Acre evening and a bit special. Nine or ten of us from five or six countries were gathered around a large table on the bar's terrace. Dado was struggling to keep us in a single conversation when his Elena suggested we play a game. We were each to say whose first name we liked the most and why. When it came to Margaret's turn, she said she liked Elena's name the most because her middle name was Eleanor, the English equivalent.

Instead of playing a third set, I walked back to Cambridge's city library and in its reference section found a book detailing contemporary novelists. Margaret Atwood's middle name is Eleanor.

Now that the ghost had returned, I decided to stay with her a bit longer. I walked up Trinity Street to Heffers, a beautiful multi-level bookshop where in my impecunious Cambridge years I had spent hours reading standing up. I recalled that up on the mezzanine there was a large poetry section. I had yet to read Margaret's poetry, and now I was going to have a glimpse. I found several Atwood volumes, picked one up, turned it over to its back cover and froze.

I have told you that although the two or three photos of Margaret Atwood I had seen were consistent with my memory of Margaret Bezan, if they had been my sole evidence I would have remained unsure about the oneness of the two Margarets. The whole of the back cover of the paperback I was holding was a black and white photo of Margaret sitting on a garden terrace with her hands, palms down, flat on the table in front of her. Unmistakably they were the pair of hands I had repeatedly admired at Happy Acre.

Simone de Beauvoir

I have explained to you how, if I had not had that late afternoon conversation up at the bar with Margaret, my life would have been unrecognizable from how it turned out to be. I would have spent it in the bank, and even if Katie and I had met, we would never have bonded. But there was still more to come from that chat with Margaret. In the nineties it again changed my life and Katie's too.

We had been together 18 years when one evening Katie and I told a dinner guest some of the story of how *The Second Sex* had brought us together. This storytelling led to us receiving a few weeks later a publisher's invitation to write a book on the literary partnership of Simone de Beauvoir and Jean-Paul Sartre.

We hesitated to accept because it didn't fit with our other projects and, since Beauvoir and Sartre were so prolific, it meant reading so many books. But when the publisher said we could have an extra year, we accepted.

We knew in advance the basic story that we would be telling because it had been told so many times and in so many languages, and since their deaths in the 1980s, half a dozen major biographies had been written. So, when we began our project, it seemed nothing new remained to be said. Except for the reading, the project didn't seem all that demanding; and for the first year and a half, Katie and I didn't talk that much about it, we just read.

But we did divide up the chapters we would write. The book would begin with one written by me on Sartre's life up until his last year as a student but before he met Beauvoir. Then there would be a corresponding chapter on Beauvoir written by Katie. Then three chapters that I would write on their first twenty years together, and then three chapters by Katie on the rest of their lives.

As I read their complete works, a problem emerged for me that got bigger and bigger. My belief in the standard story of their intellectual lives together became weaker and weaker until I was sure it was fundamentally false. The standard story was that all the ideas they shared and that constituted what was called Sartrean existentialism had come from and been developed by Sartre. Beauvoir had served only as a midwife and popularizer. But after reading all of Beauvoir's books and so much about her life, I could no longer imagine her playing for decades this passive intellectual role. But I had no hard evidence and therefore no alternative story to tell. Eventually I decided I would not be able to make myself go through with writing this book. And of course I dreaded telling Katie.

Finally, one evening at dinner, as our deadline with the publisher neared, I screwed up my courage and told Katie that I was not going to be able to write my half of the book because I no longer believed that the story we had to tell could possibly be true. Immediately, Katie's eyes filled with tears, and I thought I was hurting her even more than I had feared. But they were tears of joy. Katie said she also didn't believe the story but had been afraid to say so, knowing that Sartre was my hero.

Katie said there was a philosopher woman in the States named Margaret Simons who also didn't believe the story. I knew about Simons and had read her essay, but Katie suggested I read it again to give me encouragement. And I did. Simons had set about merely comparing the dates at which the concept of the "Social Other" (as opposed to the "Individual Other" as found in *Being and Nothingness)* first appeared in Sartre's and Beauvoir's works.

This concept, with its underlying theory, had been one of the most influential of the century, having, from the period of decolonization onwards, provided a powerful intellectual lever for liberation movements, as well as being an idea, like the Unconscious, now used in all manner of social and cultural analysis.

The invention of the idea of the "Social Other" had always been credited to Sartre, in whose post-1950 philosophy it plays a key role. Simons, however, noted that Beauvoir worked out the concept in her *The Ethics of Ambiguity* and *The Second Sex*, books published well before Sartre began to write the work in which he first used the concept.

It might seem incomprehensible that these facts, which Simons published in the prestigious *Yale French Review*, could have gone unnoticed for so long. But unlike Beauvoir's bisexuality, the discovery that a major idea of the century had originated with a woman, was found not to be noteworthy.

Sartre scholars chose to ignore Simon's incontrovertible evidence, demonstrating that there is one more right that women have not yet won. "Crediting women with major ideas," said someone at a dinner party, "is the last taboo".

I started looking in new directions for evidence of Beauvoir contributions to Sartrean existentialism. I couldn't have timed it better. Recently there had appeared four volumes of Sartre and Beauvoir documents focused on the period in question: *Sartre's War Diaries* (1985) and Beauvoir's *Lettres à Sartre 1930-1939* (1990), *Lettres à Sartre 1940-1963* (1990) and *Journal de Guerre* (1990). Soon I was reading the couple's journals and letters day and night.

Heretofore, Beauvoir's four autobiographies had established the basis of the legend surrounding her partnership with Sartre, which, in the main, was faithfully retold by the couple's numerous biographers. But now, armed with a growing appreciation of the pair's capacity for falsehood and with these letters and journals, I set about re-scrutinizing the famous relationship. Almost at once, old verities crumbled before my eyes. The truth emerged as nearly the inverse of the legend.

Contrary to the legend, Beauvoir had not been a virgin when she met Sartre in 1929, but rather the current lover of one his closest friends. It had not been Beauvoir who had initially pressed for marriage, but rather Sartre. Their agreement that they should each be allowed to have "contingent" loves had been initiated to satisfy Beauvoir's demands, not Sartre's. Soon, in addition to frequent random couplings, Beauvoir was sleeping not just with one, but with two of Sartre's best friends. And as the pair became thirty-something it was Beauvoir, not Sartre, who threatened to forsake the other for someone younger.

According to the legend, at the time of Sartre and Beauvoir's first meeting, as they prepared for their final university exams, she had been not only his intellectual equal but also had provided many of the ideas for their endless philosophical discussions. But, the legend continued, after college Beauvoir became passive in the face of Sartre's intellect and remained so ever after. Simons' discovery, however, had shown that from the mid-1940s the Sartre-and-Beauvoir legend regarding the source of their philosophical ideas had no basis in fact. Beauvoir's denial of contributing to "Sartre's" later philosophy had been a lie told for reasons I could not fathom. Perhaps she also had lied about not having originated any of the ideas in *Being and Nothingness* (1943), the primary basis of Sartre's reputation as one of the century's most important philosophers.

My research had turned up many facts pointing circumstantially to this conclusion. There were the numerous hints in Beauvoir's writing, that she had helped with the making of Sartre's philosophical system.

There was the fact that in the mid-1930s, as Sartre's interest turned away from philosophy, Beauvoir renewed her commitment to it. There were their joint admissions that Beauvoir, not Sartre, was the expert on phenomenology and that his German hadn't been up to reading Heidegger.

Instead it had been Beauvoir, they revealed in an interview in their old age, who had read the German existentialist in 1936, with Sartre reading only those passages that she translated for him. Her letters and diaries also described how she, not Sartre, read and analysed Hegel at the end of the 1930s.

Then there was the question of whether it was humanly possible to have done all that Sartre and Sartre scholars claimed he did between 17 February 1940, when he had his first original philosophical ideas, and October 1942, when he submitted his manuscript of *Being and Nothingness* for publication.

The feats claimed for Sartre in this period of 32 months include the following: read and closely analysed Hegel and Heidegger; invented from scratch his own highly original and monumental philosophical system; wrote a 700-page account of his philosophy; wrote, produced and acted in a play, wrote and published another one; wrote one-and-a-half long novels; wrote numerous articles; spent four months as soldier in an army at war; spent nine months as a prisoner of war; escaped from a German prison camp; worked for a year as a full-time lycée teacher; seduced many young women; organized a resistance movement; traveled for a whole summer by bicycle through France, and so on.

On paper Sartre looked like an intellectual Arnold Schwarzenegger character, a stereotypical male fantasy.

My own admiration for Sartre had always been focused on his existentialist philosophy as expounded in *Being and Nothingness*. As I previously hinted, reading and rereading this book was one of the key intellectual adventures of my youth. I felt gratitude towards someone whose ideas had for so long enriched my mental life. But I was apprehensive about the need now to reconsider those ideas.

In the quarter century since my Sartrean feast I had digested a lot of philosophy, most of it in the analytic tradition. Rereading *Being and Nothingness*, I was delighted to find that my youthful ardour had been so well placed. The metaphysical daring, logical strength and, above all, human relevance of Sartre's philosophical system was no less impressive than I remembered.

Hard evidence of a contribution by Beauvoir to that system had failed to materialize, as our publisher's deadline neared.

But the circumstantial evidence was so overwhelming that I no longer found remotely plausible the notion that Beauvoir had contributed nothing to Sartrean existentialism. I also felt that somewhere in the vast stack of Sartre-and-Beauvoir biographical material were the rigid facts that would nail the case.

Scholar's pride on the one hand, and on the other the hope that the last taboo might fall in our lifetimes, drove me to repeatedly re-examine the main documents. I was looking for at least a small contribution.

Sartre's *War Diaries* told us that the genesis of his philosophical system had begun, for him, suddenly and spectacularly on February 17, 1940. Only weeks before, he had written in his diary about how despite months of labouring, he had failed to come up with any philosophical ideas of his own. But on the 17th, having returned the previous morning from 11 days leave in Paris, Sartre began one of those fabled bouts of male creativity. In the next 11 days our philosopher-hero sketched in his diary the rough outline of the philosophical system of *Being and Nothingness*.

For the nth time I reread the entry of the 17th. In it, Sartre credits Beauvoir with a very minor philosophical idea. He indicated that while on leave he had gleaned this idea from her then unpublished novel *She Came to Stay*. I recalled how she had convinced her biographer, Bair, that she had written hardly any of her novel at the time of Sartre's February leave and how the letters she had left to be discovered after her death proved this to be untrue.

It took forty minutes to find the passage mid-novel from which Sartre had picked up the inconsequential concept which he named "unrealizables". I recalled that Beauvoir's diaries show that Sartre, while on leave, had at least eight reading sessions with *She Came to Stay*.

Still, I could not imagine how he could have spotted this one small philosophical nugget. Unless, of course, (as one does with his novel *Nausea* and with Plato's *Dialogues*) he had read the whole of Beauvoir's novel as a philosophical text. And then I recalled something that Hazel Barnes, the English translator of *Being and Nothingness* had written:

> Although this book (*She Came To Stay*) and *Being and Nothingness* were published in the same year (1943), the similarity between them is too striking to be coincidence. As with all of de Beauvoir's early fiction, the reader of *She Came to Stay* feels that the inspiration of the book was simply de Beauvoir's decision to show how Sartre's abstract principles could be made to work out in "real life".

But then I recalled that in phenomenology, the philosophical tradition in which Beauvoir and Sartre worked, the philosopher begins not with abstract ideas but at the level of real-life experience seeking to discover its structures which then become her abstract ideas.

I opened *She Came To Stay* at random and began reading from my new vantage point. It was a philosophical text! I turned back to page one. By the time I'd finished reading the first chapter – nine pages – I had read a succinct and lucid outline of the central arguments of "Sartrean existentialism".

Sartre in his diaries, it was suddenly clear, had merely been transcribing the philosophical system he had found in Beauvoir's novel. Sartrean existentialism is really Beauvoirean existentialism. Then from the philosophy point of view, I reread the whole novel where I found all the basic ideas further explained.

Now please note – because this is one of the main reasons I have for writing this book – that my experience in the early 1990s with Beauvoir's writing parallels my experience with Margaret's in Antigua. When the latter described her writing as "schoolgirl poetry", I readily accepted it as such and never entertained the possibility that her long hours writing it signified higher, much higher, aspirations. When I read Sartre's first novel *Nausea*, shortly after my return from my travels, I read it both as a narrative **and** as a philosophical text, and that was before I had read philosophical interpretations of it. But it had never occurred to me to do the same with any of Beauvoir's novels, even though I had been an outspoken feminist for nearly thirty years. So why was I so fucking stupid when I read *She Came to Stay*?

Because I still lived in a sexist society and culture. And like everyone else, my spontaneous sensibilities and presumptions are influenced by my daily interchange with my society and culture. Like COVID-19 and its new variants, sexism is still out there waiting to get you.

Here, written seven years after our book was published, is an Amazon review of it by Sharon Wright that describes our book's impact.

> No book on Beauvoir or Sartre has led to so much discussion, provoked such consternation or so changed the way we see these cultural icons as has Kate and Edward Fullbrook's *Simone de Beauvoir and Jean-Paul Sartre: The Remaking of a Twentieth-Century Legend*. The basis of this recently republished book (which I had the pleasure of rereading last week) is disarmingly simple. The Fullbrooks checked out Beauvoir's and Sartre's newly-available letters and diaries and found that the traditional story that says that Beauvoir constructed her first novel *She Came to Stay* on the basis of philosophical ideas she took from Sartre's essay *Being and Nothingness* is the exact opposite of the truth. Sartre only began, the Fullbrooks carefully document, to compile notes for his philosophical treatise after studying the second draft of Beauvoir's novel. The Fullbrooks also, and again drawing on the letters, make the case that it was Beauvoir's sexual promiscuity, rather than Sartre's that

initially dictated the famous open terms of their 50-year relationship. All this radical post-patriarchal revisionism, which the Fullbrooks refused to play down, was too much for many critics when this book appeared in 1994. Some reviewers were apoplectic, others deeply sceptical, and the *New York Times* twice ran long reviews warning their readers against this "feminist claptrap". ... the slow but continuing cultural shift away from presuming that women are never the source of original ideas has taken away some of the shock value of the Fullbrooks' first book. Indeed, seven years on and their impressive scholarship has never been seriously challenged. By now scores of Sartre scholars must have checked out the letters and diaries and found, to their dismay, that the Fullbrooks did not make any of it up. But although *Simone de Beauvoir and Jean-Paul Sartre: The Remaking of a Twentieth-Century Legend* through its success no longer enjoys the controversy it once did, it remains, with its compelling narrative and writerly qualities, one of the best books ever written about either Beauvoir or Sartre. Even the *New York Times* had to admit that it was a good read. For capturing the spirit of these twentieth-century giants and their extraordinary relationship, this book is yet to be beaten.

After our book was published, Katie and I received many invitations to speak at conferences, and we traveled to numerous countries doing so. Then at the end of the century as the 50th anniversary of the publication of *The Second Sex* approached, conference-type celebrations were being held all over the world. The biggest was in Paris, and for its Saturday afternoon grand finale open to the public, it rented the thousand-seat Grand Amphithéâtre de la Sorbonne. Katie and I were invited as opening speakers.

Come that Saturday, Katie and I, much too nervous to eat lunch, strolled around the Latin Quarter for what seemed like days before we headed slowly up the hill to Place de la Sorbonne and the Amphithéâtre, where we found gendarmes standing behind barricades holding back a crowd waiting to get into the Amphithéâtre. Without thinking about it, Katie and I became part of the crowd. It was still growing, and soon we were no longer at its back. Neither of us said a word, but I could feel us both becoming increasingly fearful. Finally, Katie exclaimed,

"Oh Edward, I don't belong here!"

"Neither do I."

"Hold on to me tight!"

With both arms I grabbed Katie around the waist, and she clasped my hands. But with the crowd growing and shoving, I could feel us drifting backwards, when suddenly up on the top step of the entrance a woman started shouting and pointing in our direction. I couldn't understand what she was saying, then she switched to English.

"Let them through! They are the speakers!"

Now I recognized her. She was a Swedish Beauvoir scholar whom we had met in Dublin. The crowd turned

153

around to look at us and then opened a gap, and a gendarme pulled back a barricade, and Katie and I walked through.

Our presentation came off without difficulty.

Nobodies

I had kept my no-name-dropping promise to myself and had yet to tell Katie or anyone about my knowing Margaret in Antigua. Then, about a year after *The Second Sex* celebrations, Katie was near to deciding to write a book on Atwood's fiction, and I decided that when she did, I would tell her. But before she did, she was diagnosed with breast cancer.

I was sitting next to Katie when the surgeon sitting behind his desk told her the results of the biopsy.

"What are my chances?" she asked.

The surgeon turned his eyes away and thought for what seemed a long time.

"I would say you have a 40 per cent chance to still be alive five years from now."

When, after chemotherapy, radiation and a mastectomy, the cancer returned, it attacked two areas of Katie's brain, one affecting her emotional countenance, the other her physical balance. Now she needed a walker to get around and could no longer get herself up from our mattress on the floor, so after 33 years I went out and bought us our first bed. As death came closer, Katie was asleep most hours, and at noon and midnight I would wake her up to give her twelve kinds of pills. One midnight she recalled that the first month we lived together, each night in bed before we turned out the lights, I read *Robinson Crusoe* to her. She asked me to do the same now. And of course I did, but each night the number of pages I read before Katie fell asleep decreased, and the second reading was never finished. The surgeon's prediction proved accurate. Katie died thirty months after he gave it.

****

About a year later and after a Christmas-home-alone, I started exchanging emails with a French woman who I had had as a French teacher and who after finishing her PhD in England had left her partner and moved back to Paris. On my way to an economics conference in the French Alps, I arranged to meet her for lunch in Paris. A romance immediately ensued and continued in Paris and Bristol for some months. When it ended, I found myself facing another Christmas-home-alone. I decided to go traveling in India.

I arrived in Delhi in the middle of the night, and in the morning, short of sleep, went up to my hotel's rooftop for breakfast. A British woman some years my senior was sitting alone at the table opposite, and I watched and listened to her conversing like an old friend with the waiter. By the time my coffee arrived I was fascinated with her, and we had exchanged glances. Thanks to my childhood wanderings, I'm capable of striking up conversations with strangers, and on this morning I quickly decided that I would try to do so with this woman. I thought through my opening and was about to launch into it, when she was joined by a man her age, whose face immediately told me that for many decades he had enjoyed her companionship.

That tiny experience intensified my desire to find a new life partner. A few days later there in India I met a Canadian woman who lived in the Vosges Mountains in France. In the months that followed we met up for long weekends in various countries, but it was obvious from the beginning that no deep bonding was ever going to take place. Meanwhile I was looking everywhere, enrolling in evening language classes, going to my tennis club at odd hours, even going to London for the day and hanging out in book shops and galleries. Once I answered a lonely-heart ad in *The London Review of Books*.

Eventually I lost hope. To tell you how I regained it, I need first to go back to 1980.

****

The day after Christmas in Britain is called "Boxing Day". A more killjoy name for a national holiday is almost unimaginable. But not all Brits are puritans, and, among those who are not, Boxing Day cocktail parties are a common subversion. The second year Katie and I lived in Devon, we were invited to a Boxing Day cocktail party at the house of one of Katie's colleagues, John Daniel. Cocktail parties are for me potentially nightmarish social situations, and it is not just that they require a constant shifting of my attention. Worse is that most of the time I can't hear what people are saying, not because of the deafness in my right ear, but because in my mind all the simultaneous voices blur into one. More times than I can count, I have panicked and bolted out the door, once without my coat.

But through the decades I have developed various ways of usually coping. The one that works best but is seldom operable is to spot someone standing alone off in a corner. And at this massive Boxing Day cocktail party I spotted a woman standing all alone, her back to me, in a doorway; and, like a robin who has spotted a worm, I darted over. When she turned around, I couldn't believe my luck. She was beautiful, voluptuous, maybe 24 or 25, an ironic twinkle in her eyes, elegantly dressed, and I soon learned she was Parisian. She had grown up on the Left Bank and had gone to university there.

"And me, I grew up and went to university in Nebraska." We both laughed.

"I've heard of it," she said, and we laughed again.

"And now," I said, "Plymouth? Why are you here in Plymouth the day after Christmas at this weird British thing?"

She laughed again. "Because John Daniel, who I think you know, is my partner."

"Oh my God! Then *you* are the hostess of this Boxing Day event."

I was afraid, and I think she was too, that our laughter was going to attract others, so we slid through the doorway and into a kitchen where we felt free to tell each other funny stories about the Brits. But don't get me wrong; we both loved the Brits so there was no malice in our ten minutes of laughter.

My find was named Elisa Mantin. She, her partner John, Katie and me all quickly became good friends, and over the next five years we shared many bottles of wine. Then Katie and I left Devon, and soon after Elisa left John and returned to Paris.

****

It was now 2004 and eighteen years since I had had contact with Elisa. I was going to be in Paris alone for a few days and I decided to track Elisa down. I knew that she had become a successful director/producer of television documentaries on famous writers, Salmon Rushdie for example, and I soon found her email address. Yes, she would be pleased to meet me for lunch.

We met in the lobby of my hotel on the rue Delambre. And like our first meeting at that Boxing Day party a quarter of a century earlier, we were both immediately at ease with each other. Elisa led me up to the boulevard Montparnasse and then down to the Café Select, where the waiters greeted her as a regular. Over lunch we took turns briefly recounting the last twenty years of our lives, before we came to talking about where we each were now. I had come to a big fork in my life, and I had two paths mapped out. One reasonable, the other rather preposterous. And sensibly I had pretty much decided on the former. It meant essentially that I, now 66, would retire. I would give up economics and let go of the small network of rebellion I led and relocate – at least for most of the year – to one of those expat retirement villages in the south of Spain. The other path, the preposterous one, was to expand my reform movement, turn my economics newsletter into a digital academic journal, possibly with a large readership, and write and edit more economics books. I got a little carried away describing this to Elisa, and when we finally paid our bill, the Select's dining room was empty except for us.

Slowly, we walked back down the boulevard. When we came to La Rotonde we stopped to say good-by. We were about to kiss when Elisa grabbed hold of my arms and shook me. "*Go for it, Edward.*" She kissed me, turned, and crossed the boulevard.

Thanks to her four words, I did.

But six months later I was no closer to finding a new life partner, and I thought it likely that I never would, when one cloudy summer morning sitting in someone's extravagantly large conservatory, I exchanged meaningful smiles with a woman sitting up on a mezzanine on the far side. Over the next hour we had two more such exchanges and then I stood up and left what was a strange gathering and went out and sat alone in my car. Sitting there, I knew I would see my new fascination when she left. And when she did, she spotted me and again we exchanged smiles. Then came the big test. By now you know I'm peculiar, so I can tell you this. When it comes to divining how I might get on with someone, female or male, I like to watch them walk.

As I watched her walk down the sidewalk, my heart leapt. Back in the conservatory I had learned that her name was Zita Adamson and that she was a single mother and a writer, and I drove straight home and went online and ordered for next-day delivery her most recent novel from Amazon. That was seventeen years ago. I have written most of this book in the evenings on the red velvet couch in my study with Zita sitting next to me.

And my seventies were the best decade of my life.

****

For as long as I can remember, I have had to take naps half sitting up. Whenever I forgot and went to sleep flat or nearly flat on my back, my nap would end with a horrendous nightmare, and always the same one. I would be pinned down at my shoulders and struggling unsuccessfully against I knew not what to sit up. Recently taking a nap, I forgot to prop-up my shoulders and the nightmare came as usual, but for the first time ever I saw I was pinned down by a man whose sadistic smile I had grown up with. The next day I deliberately napped flat on my back and I had nothing but sweet dreams. And so it continues.

****

On 3 November 2017 I sent this email to one of Margaret Atwood's agents.

Dear Karolina Sutton,

THE MYSTERY OF THE TWO MARGARETS

I don't have Margaret Atwood's email address. Please read my brief message to her below, and if you think she might like to receive it, please forward it to her.

Thank you, Edward Fullbrook

Once in the distant past I ate your lunch.

Dear Margaret,

I owe you a favour, and now I'm asking you for another. Once in the very distant past I ate Marg Bezan's lunch. With so much else to remember, you probably don't remember your Antigua alias, but I do and would even if decades ago I had not – on recommendation of my late first wife – read *Bodily Harm* and then in my dreams, literally, made the connection between you and you.

I was Ed back then, tall, very thin, had thick glasses and a Nebraska accent, and hawked someone else's watercolours on the beaches. These days so far as I am known, it is as an economist and a Beauvoir scholar – yes, an utterly preposterous combination. My first wife was a literary critic and my second is a novelist, and by now you can maybe see what's coming: I've written a novel whose sales might benefit

greatly from a mere mention by MARGARET
ATWOOD.

Even I realize that the odds that a novel by an
economist would merit your reading are
minuscule, but please, and this is the favour I'm
asking, have a look. It is titled *American Dreams*;
its listed author is Michael Hope. Here are its
Amazon.ca links:

<u>Kindle edition</u>
<u>Paperback</u>

Sorry, but I can't think of a signoff that seems
appropriate,

Edward

On 14 November 2017 I received this email.

> Dear Edward,
> Thank you for your email, which we shared with
> Ms Atwood's office. She believes you may have
> her confused with someone else as she has never
> been to Antigua, and isn't familiar with the name
> Marg Bezan.
>
> Best wishes, Lucy

THE MYSTERY OF THE TWO MARGARETS

Lucy Morris
Office of Karolina Sutton
Curtis Brown Group Ltd
Haymarket House
28-29 Haymarket
London SW1Y 4SP

Yes, it hurt.

Michael Hope's novel has now been republished with a change of title (*Two American Dreams*) and cover, and today, unfortunately, speaks even more to our time.

****

So, are there two Margarets or only one? For me, as the storyteller, the answer makes no difference. This story is not really about any Margaret in particular, but about those nobodies – at least at the time – who, passing casually through my life or yours, give precious gifts: Miss Montgomery's gift of a red star, the black man who made me knock on his door, the visiting aunt tempting me with life's other possibilities, the traveling carpet salesman pulling me back from the cliff-edge, the Omaha beauty in the London youth hostel who gave me her smile, Ted

Joans leading me to the existential me, Dado teaching me to accept the fact that I, like us all, was unique, Margaret pointing me towards what for me was the ultimate book and suggesting a strategy for my life, the London graduate student who dragged me into where I thought I was not supposed to be, and the Cambridge don who I had only just met inviting me to a private gathering. This book is for and about nobodies like them, who – and this is the most important point – *for no reason except goodwill*, give to nobodies like me the means to live happy lives. My life is proof that us nobodies can perform miracles on each other.

Books I have written

- *The book you have just read*

- *Market-value: Its measurement and metric*, World Economics Association Books, 2020.

- (Michael Hope) *Two American Dreams*, Literary Fiction, 2017

- *Narrative Fixation in Economics*, World Economics Association Books, 2016.

- *The Decline of the USA*, Real World Economics Books, 2012

- (with Kate Fullbrook) *Sex and Philosophy: Jean Paul Sartre and Simone de Beauvoir*, London, Continuum, 2008. Chinese edition 2018

- (with Kate Fullbrook) *Beauvoir: A Critical Introduction*, Cambridge, UK: Polity Press, 1998; and Cambridge, Mass, USA: Blackwell, 1998.

- (with Kate Fullbrook) *Simone de Beauvoir and Jean-Paul Sartre: The Remaking of a Twentieth-Century Legend*, London: Harvester, 1993. New York: Basic Books, 1994. Sidney: Harper Collins, 1995.

- *The Algebraic Structure of Exchange-value.* Unpublished

Books I have edited

- *19 Subversive Essays: from Real-World Economics Review*, World Economics Association Books, forthcoming late 2022.

- (with Jamie Morgan) *Post-Neoliberal Economics*, World Economics Association Books, 2021.

- (with Jamie Morgan) *The Inequality Crisis*, World Economics Association Books, 2020.

- (with Jamie Morgan) *Modern Monetary Theory and its Critics*, World Economics Association Books, 2020.

- (with Jamie Morgan) *Economics and the Ecosystem*, World Economics Association Books, 2019.

- (with Jamie Morgan) *Trumponomics: Causes and Consequences*, College Publications and World Economics Association, 2017.

- (with Jamie Morgan) *Piketty's Capital in the Twenty-First Century*, College Publications and World Economics Association, 2014.

- *Crash: Why it happened and what to do about it*. Real-World Economics Review Books, 2009 http://www.paecon.net/CRASH-1.pdf

- *Ontology and Economics*. London and New York: Routledge, 2009.

- *Pluralist Economics*. London and New York: Zed Books, 2008.

- *Real World Economics: A Post-Autistic Economics Reader*. London: Anthem Press, 2007.

- *A Guide to What's Wrong with Economics*, London: Anthem, 2004.

- *The Crisis in Economics: The Post-Autistic Economics Movement: The first 600 days*. London and New York: Routledge, 2003. Chinese edition 2005.

- *Intersubjectivity in Economics: Agents and Structures*. London and New York: Routledge, 2002

- *(with Christine Delphy, Sylvie Chaperon and Kate Fullbrook) Cinquantenaire du Le Deuxième Sexe,* Paris: Syllepse, 2002.

Made in the USA
Middletown, DE
02 November 2022